Memory Links

with love,
c

For Shelly and Jerry:
good reading is like good
politics, yes? Hope you enjoy.

Bill Van Wert

Memory

Links

William F. Van Wert

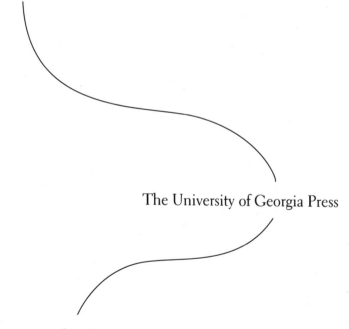

The University of Georgia Press

Athens & London

Published by the University of Georgia Press
Athens, Georgia 30602
© 1995 by William F. Van Wert
All rights reserved
Designed by Erin Kirk New
Set in 10.5 on 15 Electra
by Tseng Information Systems, Inc.
Printed and bound by Thomson-Shore, Inc.
The paper in this book meets the guidelines for permanence
and durability of the Committee on Production Guidelines
for Book Longevity of the Council on Library Resources.

Printed in the United States of America

99 98 97 96 95   C   5   4   3   2   1

Library of Congress Cataloging in Publication Data

Van Wert, William F.
Memory links / William F. Van Wert.
p.   cm.
Contents: Memory links—Georgia—The love of
narrative—Texas—Homes of memory glue—Nebraska—
The Roy stories—Maine—Homesickness—The disappearance
of setting—Michigan—Indiana.
ISBN 0-8203-1750-0 (alk. paper)
I. Title.
PS3572.A4228M45   1995
814'.54—dc20   94-48868

British Library Cataloging in Publication Data available

*Winner of the Associated Writing Programs
Award for Creative Nonfiction*

For Ian, David, and Daniel

Contents

Acknowledgments

My thanks to Nadia Kravchenko in Philadelphia for her assistance in preparing the manuscript and to Kim Cretors and Grace Buonocore for their assistance at the press.

"Georgia" first appeared in *New Letters*. "The Disappearance of Setting" first appeared in a slightly altered version in the *Ohio Review*.

Memory Links

Memory Links

Toby and I go golfing. We're both university professors, so on a nonteaching day in the middle of the week, we can be out on the links with the retirees, the corporate executives cutting deals, and the many women, young and old alike, who have taken up golf. There is this difference between women and men: women will play sports with their friends, an extension of their friendship, while men will play sports with whomever they are lucky to find at their proficiency level and time convenience, and if a friendship develops, so much the better.

I am thinking as we drive out of the city of the sports a man can play that are not team sports and that suit his changing body once he has passed the age of forty. I am a tennis player, a good tennis player, and for the most part I play with strangers, the husbands of colleagues of mine, mostly lawyers, who are also good tennis players but with whom I have very little in common. The play is fast and furious, within a confined urban space, a set time limit. The object is to get as many sets played in the two hours of court time we have paid for as we can. There are compensations. I make up for a mediocre backhand with strong serves, an accurate topspin forehand, and good net play.

Golf is the opposite. You pay for the grounds, not the time it takes to cover them. You give up the better part of a day to play eighteen holes, you take the time for practice swings, you measure the putts, you wait on people ahead of you, you spend time looking for your ball in the woods or water. Consistency is crucial in tennis, and you are always measuring your strengths against an opponent's weaknesses. One bad shot can cost a game or set or match. In golf, they speak of certain holes as "unforgiving," you're always pitted against yourself and the elements, and there is always something to be salvaged, something to keep you coming back. On a given hole, a par four, my score is eight, for example. Of the eight strokes, though, four may be as good as any I have ever made. For me, the drives and fairway shots are brilliant; the chips and putts are atrocious. I am frustrated but not unhappy.

Toby and I leave the city of Philadelphia, cross the bridge to New Jersey, and take the back roads to several golf courses with names like Ramblewood, Golden Pheasant, and Excalibur. There is time to catch each other up on departmental gossip, on the writing each of us is doing, on what we will do between semesters. And there is time to appreciate the trees of spring, the dotted landscape of disappearing farms, the signs for country auctions. People who don't play golf generally assume it's a boring sport played by boring people on land that could be put to better use. But if you have ever walked a golf course, you appreciate the wind in your face, the trees that are both beautiful sights and obstacles, the rise of a sand trap, slope of water, the manicured greens. You replace your divots, you rake the sand traps when you leave, you put flags back in the cup, and suddenly it's not a stretch to say that golfers are farmers of a sort. They till the land they cover. Nor is it a stretch to say that less than a quarter of the time spent on the links is in the actual manipulation of the woods and irons.

The rest is walking, sizing up, searching for lost balls, waiting, standing, sitting, and, yes, meditating. For me, golf is a form of walking meditation. No matter how bad my score is, the exercise is always good, the meditation even better. After eighteen holes, my body is tired, my head is clear, and living in a city becomes manageable again.

Toby and I have both written about golf, he in a novel, I in a short story, both published and collected together in an anthology that soon will be translated into Italian. We've been saying for fifteen years that we should go golfing. I remember Toby before he was a famous novelist. We were both teaching at the branch campus north of Philadelphia; I was new to the profession, he was already a veteran, and we were both teaching an evening composition class. It was break time, we were both smoking cigarettes, clouds were swirling overhead.

"A good day for golf," he said.

I agreed, even though I didn't golf then.

Growing up in Michigan, I associated golf courses with the very rich who lived near them and whose high fences protected them from errant shots. I imagined these rich people sliding out of bed in the morning and onto the links in one fluid motion, cat's sleep still in their eyes. Even then, you had to belong to country clubs to use such courses. I could drive around them but not walk on them. They were the forbidden grounds, the "eyesore" that denied me.

At night, especially on nights after rain, my brothers and I would go with a flashlight and hunt for worms for our summer fishing. We crawled on the greens on hands and knees, turned on the flashlight, and grabbed the unsuspecting nightcrawlers. Often, there were two of them together, mating. Thus, while I was denied access during the day, I was a frequent visitor at night.

Golf courses were good for fishing, a strange synesthesia of sports. Instead of pulling twigs patiently out of my putting path, I was used to ripping worms from their escape routes, often getting only the top half of a worm, while the bottom half broke free and disappeared under the manicured carpet of the greens.

Toby talks about the disappearance of trees: the sycamore, the silver linden, the bold hickory, and the Dutch elm. He says that golf courses of his youth used to be getaway places, part of a drive away from civilization, nestled away somewhere in the really rural areas, so that part of the fun was getting there. Now the wooded spaces between such courses and the suburbs with their shopping malls and fast-food strips were disappearing, spaces being cleared for development: condominium complexes, retirement colonies, medium-rise office space. Soon, the hard-to-find golf courses snuggled away in rural New Jersey will be annexes, susceptible to the invading people, cars, noise, and trash that come on the heels of every development, every time the land is laid waste.

I like it that Toby is so sensitive to the ravages of the landscape on our way to something so apparently unaware and unpolitical as a golf outing. And I realize that much of the pleasure of golf is aural, not visual. The silence is part of the game. Hearing yourself think is part of every shot. Even the sound of someone else's bad shot from another fairway banging in the trees near you is acceptable and not considered noise pollution. Someone hollering "fore" is as loud as it gets.

Another association I have of golf courses in Michigan during my childhood has again to do with sports other than golfing. After a new snowfall in winter, the golf course was always the best place to go for sledding and tobogganing, rolling down hills and building secluded snow people. The only other people there were all interested in doing the same things, and there were eighteen holes of snow, plenty of room for everyone, free of cars, snowplows, salted streets, and city trucks. The golf course was both public in a spatial way and private in a people way. The rich were off to ski, leaving the golf courses to us.

At the first golf course, Toby and I can't get a guaranteed start-up time. We don't want to wait and we don't mind driving, so we go to the next one. Here we can start up immediately, if we agree to be part of a foursome. Of course, we agree. The other two men are strangers to us, but conversation comes easily. Toby has just bought a Wilson Firestick, a graphite driver, for two hundred and twenty dollars, and the other two men ask about it, take practice swings with it, talk about their own clubs.

It's funny how you can type a golfer after only a hole or two. One of the two men playing with us is short and stocky and takes the driver all the way back behind his neck on the swing. He hits straight, hard, and far. The other man is tall and thin, clearly the protégé of the two. His swing is slow and deliberate. He barely goes behind the shoulder with it and follows through as though he were chipping. A short, delicate, compact swing, but his ball goes on a line drive, straight, hard, and far.

Toby and I are the wild cards. Toby hits for power, and his swing rises slowly from his hip to his shoulder and through, but the results with his new Firestick are mixed and erratic. He hits a major league pop-up, he tops the ball and it bounces strangely in the high grass, or he slices on a bivouac arc into the woods. I am always the fourth to hit, because I always have the highest score per hole. My drives draw praise from the strangers, even though everyone knows I will waste them with bad putts.

We move off in a hurry, sheathing our clubs in the bags, not unlike, I think, hunters today and cowboys of old might holster their weapons. We hurry to find our ball, spot the ball, choose the right club for the next shot, line up the shot, take all kinds of time to make the shot, then hurry again. This stutter-stopping "jammed flow" has a rhythm: we always follow etiquette, the farthest from the cup hitting first, the closest to the cup hitting last. The same etiquette applies to putting on the greens.

I have state-of-the-art tennis rackets but not golf clubs. I have bought my clubs over time at yard sales, on sale at pro shops, for ten or twelve dollars per club at K Mart. I have a personal attachment to drivers and putters, nothing in between. My rule of thumb is always to use odd numbers (one, three, five, seven, and nine), with a preference for woods over irons whenever possible. In my golf bag, in fact, there are no even irons: no two, four, six, or eight iron anywhere. I do have a variety of chipping clubs: a pitching wedge, a sand wedge, a dual wedge, and a chipper. I'm told that chippers are outlawed in tournament golf play, but I am terrible with a nine iron, erratic with a pitching wedge, and actually fair with a chipper, so I hang on to the chipper and avoid sanctioned play.

Greens may look carpeted, but they're anything but flat, like pool tables are. There's always a run or break to them. Frankly, I am illiterate. Golfers talk about *reading* the break of a green, and I am illiterate. The putt always looks straight-on to me.

"Tough luck," someone tells me. "Your ball didn't break right."

Luck has nothing to do with it. I might make a putt from time to time, but it's not usually because I read it right.

Reading a slope correctly can be essential to one's health. I have this memory from my high school years. Having read Edith Wharton's *Ethan Frome* in English class, I was fascinated with the attempted suicide in that novel. Ethan and his lover try to kill themselves by crashing into a tree. Instead, they are maimed for life, and the novel ends with Ethan's shrew wife taking care of both of them. Still more imitative than original, I convinced a girlfriend to go to the golf course one night in winter after a big snowfall and crash our sled into a tree. She had read the same novel in the same English class and wasn't particularly taken with the attempted suicide, but she was a good sport and agreed to do this dumb thing. We preplanned our escape routes. At the last minute I would lean left and she would lean right. That way we would be thrown off in those respective directions upon impact instead of headlong into harm's way and the tree. We succeeded in splitting the sled in two equal parts. I was thrown free to the left, but my girlfriend's hip and leg hit the tree on her way to being thrown to the right. She limped off to the car and wouldn't speak to me for a week.

"I'm not reenacting any more novels with you," she finally said.

The book we were reading in class at that time was Thor Heyerdahl's *Kon Tiki*.

Good golfers are a treat to watch on the greens. They squat over their ball, as though they had hatched it. They hold their club from the handle down, dangling it like a dowser rod. They bunch up their bodies and huddle over the ball. Such contortions and seriousness. They get behind their putt, look the ball to the cup, lean with body English to the left or right the way baseball players try bodily to turn a foul ball fair into a home run. But here the distances are a matter of inches one way or another, and a putt of three feet counts strokewise the same as a drive of three hundred yards. Good golfers, even when they miss the putt, leave themselves with a good lie, a good leave, a "gimme" close to the cup. I overswing my putts and go from one edge of the green to the opposite edge, bypassing the cup along the way.

I began playing golf at the age of forty and only then to be with my father, who took up the game at the age of sixty-five when he retired and moved to Florida. It was a way to be with my father, a way to be alone with him, away from my mother and my brothers and sisters. I didn't have the same passion for golf that he did. What I had was a desire to be around him when he was feeling passionate about something. This, too, was a memory link with my childhood, for my father and I had not played sports together since Little League days, when he would hit fly balls after supper and I would shag them until it was dark or he gave up from too much sweating, whichever came first.

My father was a Dutch farmer who had left the farm and done well in business. He cared about appearances and results. Conversation between us had slowed to a crawl, and golf reanimated the dialogue. He gave advice freely in those early days when he was teaching me, but only enough tips to help me improve, not enough to make me competitive. I realized early on that the payoff for me in these outings was a certain intimacy with my father, while the payoff for him was a victory over a younger, stronger man. He valued the drives the most, and so I got the most instruction on drives. When we didn't have time to play nine holes, we could always go to the driving range and continue the instruction. It took me many outings to realize what an impatient golfer he was. He took a lot of time on his drives, less on his fairway shots, and by the time he got to the greens, he was excited, in a hurry, and without a clue. I came by my putting illiteracy honestly. When he missed his par, he would get angry, as though somebody had done him an injustice. He seemed to quit trying on ensuing putts, and sometimes he gave himself a gimme when it wasn't a gimme, perhaps to keep his score respectable. Rarely did he say that he would give me one, that I could pick up my ball without making the near-in putt. Where he excelled in putting was on the par threes. For some reason, he kept his patience on the par threes, as though he had undergone a personality change for such holes. He commiserated with my bad putting, but he offered no tips. On those rare holes when I threatened to beat him, he even went so far as to add to the pressure.

"Show me how it's done," he would say as I was about to putt.

"Don't choke," he sometimes said.

During the two years my mother was dying of cancer, these golf outings were the only time-out times for us. He would lighten up, be boyish and surly, tell an occasional off-color joke, then sober up, go silent, and return to grim face when we returned to my bedridden mother. When my mother's condition got worse and she was hospitalized, my father and I would sometimes go from her bedside to the driving range. Unspoken between us was the understanding that we weren't there to improve our game. We were there to crush balls, hit them with all the anger we had pent up inside, slaughter them if we could. My father would sometimes whiff mightily, Casey at the bat, then stare at me in foolish red-face, like he had done an uncondonable thing. I encouraged this release of his anger, since he would allow himself no other.

My mother died, my father aged, and golf outings became a thing of the past. He couldn't get up his cheer enough to go. It was too expensive, too early or too late in the day, too many people there. Later, it was his Parkinson's that prevented him, his erratic bladder, his fear of being too far away from toilets. He still carted his clubs with him, Florida in the winter, Michigan in the summer, but he no longer used them.

He has this newspaper clipping on his dresser in the bedroom. The clipping announces that he got a hole in one several years ago on a course in Florida. Never mind that it was a par three. My father is as proud of that clipping as any of his business awards and trophies. In his short-lived golf career, he got a hole in one.

The clipping announces the names of the people who were in his foursome that day. Like the survivors of a deceased person in an obituary, I think, reading his clipping.

For years, then, because he didn't golf, I didn't either. My golfing had been set up that way, the summer outings with my father, my golfing to coincide with his golfing. Unlike other sports, I never assumed that I might continue playing without him. And only when I turned the corner of my youth and knew that I was fully middle-aged did I think of golf again.

I still wonder why the game is associated with white people, with rich people, and with middle age on into the twilight years. Or even that it's a male sport. Most of these stereotyped associations are no longer valid. Maybe TV golf reinforces them, all those straight-arrow, close-cropped men in logo shirts and white belts and gridlock polyester pants and the droning British and Australian accents who comment on them and make stale jokes about their own game. Golf has to be the most boring and tedious of TV sports, exciting only for the intermittent aerial shots of trees or coastline before cutting to commercial.

It's a blessing for Toby and me. Out of the city and away from the stress of living in our heads all the time, we enjoy being older men in a timeless, pruned environment. I suggest meekly to Toby that when they named his graphite driver Firestick, maybe they meant kindling. He makes fun of my K Mart clubs. We remember the past freely as we play. Soon, he will play daily on a course at the Cape in Massachusetts, and I will teach summer school every day, with no time to play. We both appreciate the passage of time to this ritual. After eighteen holes, the body is tired and glad to sit down, but the mind haunts and persists in holding the holes a little longer. We've both broken a hundred, so there is nothing to be proud of in our scores. And yet we're both calm, at peace this sun-drenched Thursday in May. On our way back to Phila-delphia, we stop at one of those throwbacks, an A&W root beer drive-in, the kind we both used to cruise as high schoolers with fresh licenses. It seems somehow fitting to me that we're both lick-ing the foam from our lips as we cross the Ben Franklin Bridge and enter the city of all our duties and responsibilities again.

Georgia

My best memories of being married have to do with walking through Georgia woods on late summer afternoons, walking barefoot over dry pine straw to the lakes stocked with bream and surrounded by stumps, leftover cypress knots like so many imaginary elbows and kneecaps. We walked barefoot, my ex-wife and I, but we were always mindful of snakes and poison ivy, so that we were always slowing down, stepping over things, stopping so that she could taste mint leaves or wild berries. Squadrons of doves or quail were scared into flight at our coming, the dry pine straw crackling underfoot and giving us away. The birds flew off left to right or right to left, so that their whole flight fanned out before our eyes, never straight over us or away from us. Nutrias sometimes worked the dam or jumped back into hiding, and even though we knew what they were, we always imagined them to be something else, something dangerous like baby bears or raccoons or something that might attack us. Gunshots echoed, the sounds of hunters in nearby woods, each stretch of woods both owned as personal property the closer you were to the house and shared as common hunting and fishing ground the farther away you got from the house. Even on dry humid days, things off the ground and in the shade from the sun kept their moisture and were damp with kudzu moss and thick with gnats. If you turned a pinecone the wrong way, a hundred gnats might fly in your face.

No matter how far back into the woods we went, we could still hear the rumble and exhaust of pickup trucks, so that roads, even ones we never saw, were always nearby and circling through the woods. Out there on the highway, tourists on their way to Florida sped over hills flanked with red clay, sparkling rows of pines, occasional signs for catfish or fresh tomatoes. Black families sold vegetables off the backs of flatbed trucks, the children playing tag or ball near the body of the truck, the mother arranging the wares or sitting in the cab of the truck, the father off at a distance, off in the shade, lying in a patchwork hammock that went up every morning and came down every night. It seemed to me their eyes were more bloodshot than people's eyes up north. Here in South Georgia, the state so long that natives kept the "south" not as directional marker but as pride of distinction, a way of not being Atlanta, for example, there was something in the crisp thick air, all air and no industry or pollutants, something primitive and wild yet tired and run down about the landscape, fresh azaleas and mimosas competing with pocked asphalt and rusty trucks. I imagined that people here thought of nearby Florida as a faraway place, that they "kept to home" and didn't mingle, that some of them may still not have heard how the Civil War turned out. Time itself was succulent here, ripe to overripeness, the way the smells of homemade bread swarm a kitchen long before the actual sight of any risen loaf.

My ex-wife had seemed a little strange to me in graduate school up in Indiana, and she had brought me home to Moultrie, Georgia, not just to meet her parents and get away from the rigors of our studies but also to get me to understand, the place as a proof for who she was, to "naturalize" herself in my eyes. I had been to places like Paris and Moscow and Madrid on various exchange programs, and I had felt less estranged in those foreign cities than I felt here in Georgia.

The stereotypes that "Yankees" carry of the South were all there, if that's all I wanted to see. The familiar "y'all" and Baptist drawl of shopkeepers were there in town. Circular fans barely moved the air over irregular wooden floors in stores that sold clothing whose style and colors I hadn't seen in years. Poor people shuffled the clean streets around the town square in suspenders. Merchants were polite but not helpful. They didn't get up when I came in. They noted a Yankee accent, I could see that in their eyes, but they didn't ask any questions, such as Where do you come from? or Where are you going to? Sometimes, they left their stores unattended, wide open for anyone to walk into or out of, while they met for Coca Colas with other merchants at the corner Rexall Drugs, fanning themselves with postcards or rolled-up newspapers. The poor seemed to walk the sidewalks, as though it were their job in life to do just that, the look and smell of grain elevators on them, but no homes in sight, while the rich had incredible spreads at the outskirts of town and farther still, and when they came to town, it was always for a purpose and not for long. Black people were like occasional commas in otherwise white paragraphs. The Baptist and Presbyterian churches were major landmarks, as though they had gotten first pick of lots when the town was laid out. The Colquitt Hotel was the major landmark on the square, folks going there to eat rather than take a room. And farther out, near the grain elevators, there was the Brazier Dairy Queen for high school kids to call their own, encircle with cars, and see who was who and what was what. My ex-wife noted every little building we passed in the car, even the Sunset Elementary School she had attended, as though these buildings were memory vaults and held clues to whole identities. I never would have thought to show her my grammar school in Michigan, but then Michigan for me was the place where my parents remained, not in any way the defining dossier of who I was. People from the South keep the South with them wherever they go, and it doesn't seem to matter how long they've been gone, they never totally become assimilated. In that respect at least, it seemed to me, the South won the Civil War, and conversely the North lost, because it disappeared almost instantly after the war. We speak of the Northeast, the Midwest, the Plains States, all of these regional coalitions that made up the North during the Civil War, but the North as any meaningful designation disappeared after the war.

My best memories of being married are lodged in the miles of woods behind the house they called Red Pebble Farm, in the daily walks we took down to the lake, in having her explain to me the various flowers, ferns, and ivies we encountered. For me, the walks meant making love. Sooner or later, somewhere near the lake where we could pitch a blanket and not be seen by occasional twin-prop Cessnas overhead, we would strip down and make wonderful love, then dip our feet in the lake and walk back for supper.

Her parents and the grounds around them were a territorial mix along gender lines. Her mother was a beautiful formal woman from Illinois, who had long since taken on the lilting speech of her surroundings. The interior of the house was all her domain, filled with fine furniture and fancy antiques. And the grounds adjacent to the house were hers as well, the sacred place for lawn trimming, weeding, picking up fallen pinecones, and growing all sorts of flowers all year round. The garage, on the other hand, belonged to the father, whose accent was so thick I couldn't understand him for the longest time (it seemed to me he was speaking with mashed potatoes or grits in his mouth and was doing it on purpose to keep me off balance). The garage was only nominally a place to store cars. It held all sorts of fishing poles, bait containers, shotgun shells, camouflage hats and coats, an entire woodsman's wardrobe. Behind the garage were the dog pens, and the dogs were "liberated" every afternoon to wander the woods while he fished or they were put to work when he hunted. The path to the lake was his as well, and he kept one old Buick Skylark with over two hundred thousand miles on it just for getting to the ponds with his gear. It bore all the scratches of countless trips, and it seemed gutted out inside, the spare tire gone from the trunk to make more room for the guns and poles, the whole of the interior smelling like fish and worms, the upholstery long since rotted away.

He would come home from his trips as a uniform salesman, get out of his suit and tie, put on overalls, and head for the pond with the dogs. What he shot or caught we ate. He cleaned the birds, he pointed out the places filled with shot to avoid eating, he filleted the fish, and steamed the bass slowly over coals and an empty coffee can now filled with bubbling beer to flavor the fish. The mother prepared the onions, tomatoes, black-eyed peas, all the side dishes. We all cleaned up afterward. Soon after that, the parents went to bed, always, it seemed to me, too soon after eating and just when the night was getting interesting with sounds of crickets and various animal calls, when the breezes came up out of nowhere and seemed to splash their way through the pines. Often, I would stay up later than anyone else, go outside, and unbutton my shirt, and since I was too afraid to walk to the pond in the dark, I would walk the pine-straw driveway out to the road and back.

It became clear to me that southern women ruled their houses like a kingdom, extending their domain to the flower beds outside, but they had little to do with the garages, dog pens, or hunting and fishing in the woods, and that the men, when their workday was done, were still not long for home but needed, even required, the fishing and hunting time until supper and darkness. Grocery bills were certainly kept to a minimum by the fact that they ate what they caught or killed. Up north, meals of catfish and bass, dove, quail, and duck, these were delicacies, rare and exotic treats. Here in Georgia they were the staple. I would learn that the father had lost his taste buds from a neck injury he sustained playing professional baseball, but it never stopped him from eating whole-heartedly and heavily and wanting seconds. His memory of what the food once tasted like must have been very acute.

What my ex-wife wanted to show me, without ever actually saying so in words, was that she had grown up, not in the womanly domains of the kitchen and flower gardens, but out there beyond the territorial lines, off in the woods and around the ponds. She had been her father's constant companion on afternoon fishing trips, she had gone along with the dogs on hunting trips, she had been the stand-in son her father never had. It wasn't just the South she had to show to me but the fact that she had grown up more male than female, more alone and on her own than well kept or schooled in southern belle-ism, more at home among the scattered cypress knobs than with the tiptoe care she had to have among her mother's antiques. Home, the inside of the house, had always been a showcase, a museum of fine things gotten elsewhere and brought back to stay, but real home, the place where one lets down one's hair, was beyond the lawn line where the menfolk went with guns and poles to get away and be men and gather them-selves up before coming back in darkness to be providers and cooks and family members. I think she meant to tell me she had left the South precisely for that reason: because, by sex, she couldn't ever lay claim to the wild woods she knew so well, and because, by habit and experience, she could never quite fit in with the more restricted domains of kitchen and garden. She was not a fine thing to be kept, an expensive antique to showcase and polish up for occasions. Rather, she was wild herself, wild even to herself, unpredictable as quick rain and meant for roaming, staying on the move like the nutria, building dams and then leaving them. She was, finally, a homeless person, more at home in a walk in the woods than in any rented room or apartment we took.

She grew up to resemble her mother, but under the skin she belonged to her father, territorially so, every bit as much as the garage, the dog pens, and the path to the pond. She never learned to do perfectly the "masquerade" of makeup; there was always a bit of lipstick out of place, a strand of hair that wandered off, a choice of collar or belt that didn't quite go with the rest of the ensemble. On the other hand, she could make herself up perfectly in painter's pants, denim jeans, baggy sweatshirts, camping clothes.

She was always restless with the arrangement of furniture, moving things around on a monthly basis. She treasured things she'd found on the street or gotten for a "steal" at yard sales, and whether or not they matched what we already had didn't matter to her. She backed away from machines and fancy gadgets like TV, stereo, cameras, and the like, considering them too artificial, too soulless. She was a manic gardener, but it was as much for the pleasure of spending hours outdoors than for what actually bloomed.

And when we went to Georgia to visit, she was more vigilant about approval and displeasure than I was. She waited anxiously for her mother to comment on the few extra pounds put on, the way her slip showed at church, how she would look better in contacts than in horn-rimmed granny glasses. The mother who had always sent her out to the woods to play as a child now had no grown-up company in the kitchen. My ex-wife was still the favorite fishing partner of her father, and I was treated as a know-nothing city slicker who needed to be taught how to scull quietly, how to bait my hook, how to cast along the shoreline without getting my line caught in the weeds. She and her father never expected me to catch anything, and I never disappointed them. The same general area of the pond, the same poles, the same kind of bait, and I was always the one waiting and watching, while they caught fish. "It's a good thing y'all live up north," her father said once, "because you'd starve if you had to depend on your catching supper." When I agreed, I think he finally took to liking me. I would never catch the fish he caught or run the dogs like he could. I would never usurp his domain; his place was safe in memory and in fact. But when I told my ex-wife how lucky she was to have grown up there, she looked away and said I had no idea how much of a burden it had been. It was true. I had no idea. I was oblivious to the seemingly innocent observations that were secret slurs, to all the dense dry beauty that could be cloying and overpowering with its suffocation and loneliness. I had no contract with these people, no roots in this land, and so I could appreciate all its strangeness naively, without being taken in. Once her father offered to get me a job selling uniforms if we would move down there. I declined politely and thought it was a nice gesture on his part, but my ex-wife informed me that he was making fun of what I did for a living. I don't know. If she knew the "inside skinny" and chose to take it that way, then that was her choice and her curse. I preferred to miss the nuances and enjoy the visits. I grew to like the father's accent and quirky sense of humor. I knew some of the more racial jokes were for testing me. I let them pass, slide over me, and instead of protesting or talking politics or anything else controversial, I plied him with questions about his youth, his baseball days, stories of big fish he'd caught and even bigger ones he'd missed. And when I had gotten him to loosen his tongue and tell his tales, I had also gotten him to loosen his judgments as well. I wasn't there often enough, wasn't good ole boy enough, ever to be considered as the son, but I think he "cottoned" to me, took to liking me after all. He had grown up with three sisters for siblings, had married, and had two daughters. His family had always been women, him surrounded by women, and so I think he was grateful for whatever man talk he could get, and in later years we fished without my ex-wife along.

I began to see that he and my ex-wife were opposites: he, with his professional baseball career and then his salesman job, had always been sent away from home, cast adrift in major cities up north, and all he ever wanted to do in his heart was catch bass and shoot quail. He led a complicated life, but he was really quite simple inside. On the other hand, my ex-wife, who came from the same roots, was always restless and ready to move on, not just from Georgia but from any place we were at for longer than two years. She was attractive and blond and full of southern belle charms, which she used, even if she never owned them. She liked meeting new people and talked easily on a surface level about a variety of topics. She was born to be the salesperson her father was and hated being. And if she presented a simple enough exterior, her inside life was quite complicated, always in flux or crisis, quite tormented. She wanted me to be as suffocated in the South as she was, to replay the rootlessness with her, to agree with negative rationalizations for why we could never live here or anywhere else, and when I thrived and prospered, relaxed and enjoyed myself, she found it cruel of me and held it against me.

There were many reasons why the marriage finally collapsed, most too complicated to make any sense here. But I never regretted her, especially the early years with her, and I am grateful for Georgia. I have no reason to go back now. The marriage is over, her father has died of Alzheimer's, her mother has sold the farm and moved into town. But it's still a place I think about and sometimes dream of. Sometimes, I remember the walks to the lake, how easy it was to pitch a blanket and make uncomplicated, passionate outdoors love with my ex-wife. I remember the taste of mint leaves and wild berries, the mad rush of spasmodic dogs let loose from their pens, the taste of bream soaked in beer, and the female pinecones, always more female than male, lying in the driveway like so many hand grenades. And I have this fantasy in my private Georgia of going alone to the pond, sculling without making ripples out to the deepest part of the pond, quietly dropping anchor, lighting a cigar to keep the gnats away, and casting. I have never caught anything yet in this fantasy, but I don't mind, because catching something means having to go in. I'm not really there for the fish, the fish are just what you have to pretend to be catching so that you're not found out to be a poet, a man of reverie, an idler; I'm there for the time, the good feel of sitting still in a boat on a pond where quiet itself is a kind of singing and the only condition on the time is the setting of the sun. So far, in my fantasy it has never set.

The Love of Narrative

Truth be told, some of us look for writers who let us out of our skins just long enough to occupy the train ride to work, the hour to kill before dinner, the twenty minutes before falling asleep. We go to genre writers for this, best-sellers, books we're done with when we're done. But the writers who touch our souls are the writers who seem to take us bodily where they are, and we never regret the time we are gone from our surroundings; writers who can make us cry about characters we'll never meet but feel we know and would recognize at the grocery store or laundromat if we saw them; writers who can make us laugh about the most insignificant things, like ordering from a menu in a foreign language or struggling with the complexities of traffic signs or coming to terms with our inability to use the simplest tools around the home; and writers who can take us out of the doldrums of a gray February day and give us an uplift, a smiling wisdom about what it is to be human.

These writers have names for each category. For lyrical travel accounts, a John McPhee. For nostalgia about the past, a Russell Baker; for wicked satires about our foibles, a Calvin Trillin; for smiling wisdom, a Richard Rodriguez or Scott Sanders. These names become for us like totems; once we find one we like, we read everything else written by that writer. Not so different from the way our children collect baseball cards or trade Nintendo games. They, too, have their own quest of favorite writers. My ten-year-old son wants every book ever written by Roald Dahl, especially now that he has recently died, and not just to read, but to own and to have, to collect side by side and make precious space for on a crowded bookshelf. The girls in his class feel the same way about Judy Blume. My twelve-year-old son has collected all the historical novels of Lloyd Alexander. My fourteen-year-old is in the thrall of Stephen King and Richard Bachman, the two-in-one obsession. At their age I was collecting all the Chip Hilton sports novels written by Clare Bee.

I remember feeling embarrassed by how much I loved *Lorna Doone* in high school. The novels of James Fenimore Cooper or Hawthorne would have been more "male" and, so, more acceptable, but *Lorna Doone?* I remember being torn apart by Edith Wharton's *Ethan Frome*, so much so that I talked a girlfriend into crash-landing a toboggan into a tree on a snowy Michigan golf course one February night. She had read the same book in the same class and didn't feel the same need to replicate fiction in life, but she was a good friend and went along for the ride. One lazy high school teacher spent an entire semester reading Thor Heyerdahl's *Kon Tiki* out loud to us, cover to cover, and while other students passed notes to each other, daydreamed, prepared for other classes, or looked out the window, I was captivated by the nerve of those men, the almost religious faith it must have taken to leave land voluntarily and go forth on a raft, losing weight, growing beards, eating fish, getting sunburned and storm tossed, and all the while holding out hope that sooner or later they would arrive, get there, find land again. I may have been the only one that teacher was reading to, but I was glad for that semester and remember it better than all the other English classes in which we used yardsticks and diagrammed sentences and ran roughshod through twenty plays of Shakespeare in ten weeks. It reminded me of being read to as a child at bedtime, of hearing someone tell a story around a summer bonfire, of listening to those old radio classics before they were considered classics.

Beyond what's pulp and what's great books, beyond what's high-brow and what's low, what counts for me here is the love of narrative in all its forms. My sons love to read the tabloids at the supermarket (they call them the "scabloids"), all those stories of Adam and Eve found in Asia or First Grader Expelled for Growing a Beard. Similarly, I like to read local newspapers for what fills the dead pile, those capsule stories that complete a column on page ten or fourteen. This love of narrative can come from anyone and often comes from the most unlikely sources, not necessarily the greatest teachers or best storytellers. I remember a particular teacher I had for Freshman Composition at the University of Michigan, a wild man who expressed no love for his students, called us "dummies" after dreaded pop quizzes, and was known to throw chalk or erasers at people who slept or weren't paying attention. He frowned a lot, his glasses kept sliding down his nose, he was left-handed, and his aim wasn't particularly good. That's what I remember about him. I imagine now that he was a graduate student, beset with financial problems and the frustrations of writing a dissertation, stuck in our class of Freshman Comp. He didn't teach us anything about composition; instead, he did "readings." And I remember him saying, just before we started reading Dostoyevsky's *Crime and Punishment*: "I envy you virgins this first time. I remember reading this book for the first time, and I envy you that feeling." We were all shocked at being called "virgins," and his sentence was probably soon forgotten by most of the students in the class, but I never forgot it. In that one sentence, this sour man exposed a world of passion, and I wanted into that world. I wanted my piece of that passion. I remember not particularly liking the religious conversion of Raskolnikov at the end of that novel, but I sat back proud at the end of the book, thinking I was one of the initiated now, and I could envy everyone else who hadn't yet read it.

Every time I hear that song by Willie Nelson and Waylon Jennings, "My Heroes Have Always Been Cowboys," I keep the tune but change the words in my mind, for my heroes have always been writers. Having met a good many of them, who turned out to be drunkards or boasters or womanizers or insecure narcissists, has not changed my mind, for the mind keeps the ideal, not the reality. I didn't have to keep the totality of that wild man throwing chalk in Freshman Comp., just the one pearl he said. But where did that love of narratives come from? It didn't come out of my particular gene mix, out of thin air, or out of a Chinese fortune cookie. It had to come from somewhere.

Strangely, it came from my father, my silent Dutch father, the same one who once told me I puzzled him because I had gotten more schooling than any of his seven children and I became a teacher and a writer, and what was I good for? Money talks and something else walks. That was his motto. He had an almost eerie reverence for my younger brother who became a lawyer. So, it would come as a shock to him to know that he gave me the love of narratives.

Here's how. He was a farmer's son, who left the farm at sixteen, sold tomatoes on the roadside, saved and saved, eventually earning enough to put himself through business school. Insecure about his farmer speech, he used the dictionary every night, memorizing five to ten words a night, words he would then use and make part of his everyday speech. Just like the tomatoes, he dealt in dictionary words, one by one, saving and saving, finally making them his own. He told us this story over and over; we could have stopped him at any point, we knew the story by heart. And just as my older brother, the would-be priest, used to say Masses in the bedroom, giving out Necco wafers for communion, my imaginary passion was language. I didn't use the dictionary like my father. Instead, I memorized names from the phone book and wrote little two-page stories incorporating those names I found that were the most difficult to spell, usually Polish or Ukrainian names. And I read an outdated book of torts from some neighbor's law school days that was passed on to us when the neighbor moved, all those short short stories, a paragraph or two at most, involving the most heinous crimes and interesting trials and surprising punishments. I didn't care about legal precedents; I read for the plots. And it seemed to me strange and wonderful that the same word applied both to stories and burial grounds, and ostensibly under the pretense of sneaking somewhere to smoke a cigarette, I went with friends to cemeteries when I was in high school, and while the others were there for the smoke and telling gossip, I was memorizing the names on the headstones and imagining their lives by the weird inscriptions on the stones: infants who had to have been crib deaths, old patriarchs who were revered as gods, husbands and wives who were best beloved and endeared unto eternity. The stuff of heroism and whole sagas reduced to a catch-all phrase on those stones. The Bible was a big overstuffed book of torts and plots for me; I loved all that begatting and siring unto someone that kept prolonging the stories and spreading out the tribes and families. When my mother couldn't afford the so-called classics, she bought us the comics, the Classics Illustrated of Mark Twain and Robert Louis Stevenson. More torts and plots and names to memorize.

I developed a photographic memory for names, and I suppose I could have pleased my father greatly if I had become a lawyer with this memory for names. I could have recited precedents until I was blue in the face. But I didn't want the actual outcomes of cases or the tedium of time it took to resolve them or the protocol and jargon of the legal profession. I wanted to extract those people from their cases, give them new torts, and watch them wriggle and dangle until some new conclusion could be imagined.

I see that same imagination at work in my sons. When they were younger, they would hold He-Men or Transformers in their hands and imagine derring-do situations for them, complete with plots and dialogue spoken in shrieks or mechanical voices or threatening monotones, often prolonged and stretched into serials or sequels when the car trip we were taking was a long one. Often, their homemade stories were better than the eventual spin-off Saturday morning cartoons of He-Men, transformers, Teenage Mutant Ninja Turtles, or Nintendo characters, and they themselves instinctively knew their stories were better, because I have seen them turn off such cartoons and go to their bedrooms, and heard their voices making up new dialogue that had nothing to do with selling product and was never interrupted by commercials. I would argue that this form of play is akin to reading books, not the killer opposite or death of reading or threat of illiteracy that many people contend. This play comes from the love of narratives. Remembering my own childhood filled with dreaded hours of practicing piano scales leading up to actual lessons, I now think music could be taught much more creatively if teachers sometimes asked their pupils to invent their own scales, simulate emotions with the keys, tell stories through the free play of chords, instead of the rote ritual of mathematical scales, the forced learning of diminished and augmenteds. Teach children to tell a misadventure in minor chords leading up to studying Bach; let children brag and boast by free-play wandering between B flat, E flat, and A flat as a prelude to studying Beethoven. At the very least, tell them you envy this, their first time with a Bach or Beethoven piece.

My own best moments spent in the sciences were ones in which I could create narratives. Biology for me was the love of creating elaborate gene charts, mixing as many as ten dominant traits with ten recessive traits and then figuring out the chances of getting this or that kind of baby. Math for me was probability theory, playing out odds and chances for card games, ball games, lottery picks, all those narrative backdrops with which I housed the disembodied numbers. And history for me wasn't just the memorizing of wars and Crusades and plagues and pretender Popes but also getting a fix on the names of the Hapsburgs and Hohenzollerns, imagining their inbreeding and court jealousies, thinking up stories about them that weren't in the books. In my college notebooks, as I re-read them, the actual theories are often missed or sketchily gotten, but the examples are meticulously annotated; often, there are extras in the margins, examples I must have thought of on the spot, ones not mentioned by the professor. This is the love of narrative.

Somewhere along the line in our language acquisition and formal schooling, we lose (or maybe just misplace) the love of narratives. We think of narratives as storytelling, an art form, something that takes a lot of imagination, hard work, energy, and we don't think we can create anymore, we don't think we can be that amusing or entertaining or interesting. The awareness of boredom, that hairy monster that hits all teenagers and reduces them to saying "like" before every third word, means not only that we can be bored but also that we can be boring. My experience with teenagers is that they all secretly believe they are boring, because they all know they are bored. The love of narratives has gone out of their lives.

When my boys were little, I used to tell them bedtime stories in the dark about when I was a boy. We called them "Roy stories," because they were always about me and Roy, and Roy was always the one who got us into trouble, the tall-tale boy, the liar, the butt of the joke. Most of the stories were humorous, stories about me one-upping Roy, and the laughter my boys had at the end relaxed their bodies, so that they surrendered to my back pats and massages, they gave in to my kisses, and they were often half-asleep or already snoring when I left the room. Over time they developed their favorites, and of course they asked me to retell the one about the farmer's dog or getting lost in the woods or snagging a tennis sneaker instead of a bass while fishing. And of course I could never retell them, because they were made up in the first place and I didn't remember. Now as teenagers they still ask for the Roy stories, even though by now they know the stories are tall tales, not because those stories still hold the same interest or wonder for them (they're surely not as funny as Roald Dahl nor as scary as Stephen King), but because the stories are a memory trigger of something good and safe from their childhood, of back pats and kisses they no longer accept so easily but somewhere remember in their bodies as something best beloved and endeared and treasured, of a past they can no longer touch or speak to or speak for. Maybe they envy the first time they ever heard those stories, and while the repetition of them can never reproduce the original wonder and amazement, the triggering at the root of all repetition can swarm them with another kind of wondering and amazement, one in which their own minds are cocreating, free playing, editing and abridging the fatherly voice.

There are very few things in life that can't be made into narratives. Shopping lists can be made into narratives: the ordering, the prioritizing, the failing, the attaining, the uses of things gotten. The films of Peter Greenaway turn alphabets into narratives. *Sesame Street* makes stories out of basic numbers. The concept of irrational numbers is an invitation for older children to make narratives. Phone books and junk mail and income tax returns are all conducive to narrative. Anything accessible to language is accessible to the love of narratives. Nietzsche once said that "man is the beast who makes promises." Forgetting here the will to power, I want to say that "making promises" is a form of storytelling. It's what makes us forget that we are beasts, long-necked brooding cows who chew dirt rather than look at each other or at the sky. It's what we do best for each other, what makes us most human to each other, what invigorates the body beyond the blood and nerves and muscles, what we can keep of those who've changed, grown older, left us, or died. Words, all words, the words were made flesh for this very reason.

Texas

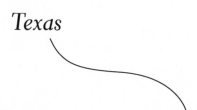

Texans indeed are a breed apart, a mestizo mix of hard German bloodlines, staunch patriarchal beliefs, the stubborn Mexican willpower they overran, cattle, oil, and vast desolate landscapes that either drive them mad or make them strong, sometimes both. The men will tell you they're a breed apart, loud and proud in foreign countries (anyplace outside Texas is a foreign country), their hair matted from too many tall hats, their lips thin from toughing it, their string ties and gaudy belt buckles, the way they smell like leather and aftershave, the way they attack a chair when they sit down, as though it were a horse, their legs straddled as to a saddle, the way they say "yessir" to strangers, their strong, unblinking eyes showing no emotion at all until the punch line, the way they bet heavily on all sports, the way they laugh and guffaw from the gut, then suddenly go grim again. The men will tell you. The women sometimes show you. Within that breed apart, they themselves are a breed apart. They range from the very rich, women whose bodies are like hobbyhorses for jewels, their skin the texture of Camay soap, the look of statuary all about them, to the renegades, the ones who rebelled and took their rancor to other states, only to discover over time they're still Texans under the surface. Both types of women are haunting, by fate and design. It's as though they can't help but show their strength, no matter how much makeup and manners they put on. They have all seen horses born and whole cities die. They have all eaten homegrown steaks over mesquite fires. They have watched their men shoot armadillo for fun, as though the animals were skeet that couldn't pull and fly. They have heard coyote howl, they've been in cars as they hit the bump gates of ranches, they know what loneliness and loyalty are. Most of them have been "outside," either as tourists or as exiles, and most of them have returned, either glad or repentant. Being Texan is like being Jewish or Catholic. If you're born to it, you can never lose it. It follows you around like a birthmark, a mole in the wrong place, an invisible posse that shadows you wherever you go.

My best friend in Philadelphia, a librarian named Gail, was one of the renegades. She came out of Texas as though it were her "birthwrong" and curse. Her older sister stayed and suffered, tried and suffered, and finally committed suicide. Gail got her college degree from Texas Tech and left the state. She went to Poland, came back with a Polish husband almost as stubborn as her father, and was informed in no uncertain terms that this foreign husband would not be part of any family inheritance. Gail and her husband came to Philadelphia. The marriage lasted several years, then collapsed, without any children. All this time her father showered money on his sons and their various financial ventures, failures, and gambling debts. And even though Gail did well enough on her own to rise to a top-level management position within the city's library system, to buy a nice house and in all material ways do well for herself, she had "failed" in the family sense: she had left the state, she had no husband, she had produced no heirs. On the other hand, she had literally *survived* by leaving; she had prospered well enough to take every imaginable tourist trip (safari in Kenya, boating down the Amazon, tiger watching in India), to buy herself a time-share in Cancun and go skiing every year at Snowbird in Utah. Still, like other rebellious runaway Texan women of her generation, she learned very early on that life wasn't fair, especially not for the so-called fair sex, and she went away angry, with a chip on her shoulder that would take years to chisel down to the size of an epaulet. The Peter Finch line from the movie *Network*—"I'm mad as hell and I'm not going to take it anymore"—would seem to such women a stock motto, elsewhere an outrageous scream.

The horror stories of her childhood are numerous. I remember this one as typical. Gail's father built a swimming pool behind the house, but Gail didn't know how to swim. The father said he would give her a lesson. He picked her up and threw her into the pool, telling her to sink or swim. She made her way to the edge of the pool. To this day, she still will not go swimming in a pool.

But what is also typical of this story, even as she admits that a parent shouldn't do such a thing to a child, is that she can never quite condemn her father.

"He taught hard lessons," she says, "and by God they made me strong."

They also made her a nonswimmer for the rest of her life, but she doesn't seem to see any tragedy in this.

The tragedy is rather in the luck of the draw, the delicate dispersal of chromosomes: if she had been born male, she would have done her Daddy proud. She was born to be a boss, never a follower. She is strong willed, stubborn, charming enough to get others to come around to her point of view. Books have been her passport through life. She reads voraciously, is ever curious, always self-taught. She has read too much to take too many lessons from others. "That's just the way I am," she says, breaching no changes. She has a passion for business and a good head for money, so much so that she might have been one of the leading oil barons of the state if she had been born a man and brought to the wells. She's wonderful with children, fiercely devotional to animals. She would have made a terrific mother as well, if she had had any children of her own.

I have trusted her completely from the moment I first met her. I think she mirrors my father for me, a kind of companion "maleness" (for lack of a better word) with which I am comfortable, at ease, secure. We have these affinities: when I get sick, I know she too is getting sick. When she gets a telephone call from someone out of her past, I too can expect such a call out of my past. When we hold hands, the fit is more than a gloved match; it's as though I am holding my own hand in the person of her hand, my own hand mirrored or doubled, and so, of course, the fit is perfect. We are thus "family" to each other. I suspect we are also "soul mates," if such a thing exists, and if such a thing as reincarnation also exists, then we have gone around together many times, perhaps as twins, maybe as brother and sister, parent and favorite offspring, husband and wife, intimate and intertwined.

But in this life I know that what makes her, of all the piebald recipe ingredients that go into making up a person, is Texas: not the Texas of *The Last Picture Show* or *Tender Mercies*, film narratives through which I have stereotyped and guessed at Texas from a distance, but a Texas deeper down and in the blood. As long as we have known each other and as intimate as the friendship has been, she has an instant common bond with any other Texan that I cannot touch or hope to understand. It may be superficial or it may be deep, I cannot tell, so much am I on the outside of it.

I have been to professional conferences in Dallas and Houston.

I can point to the grassy knoll in Dallas or speak about the glass elevators at the Hyatt in Houston, but these do not qualify me to speak about this state. But nor would I be any more qualified if I lived the rest of my life in Texas. I wasn't born there, didn't grow up there, was not formed there, and so I would always be on the outside.

But I am to be brought to the inside anyway. Gail decides for her fiftieth birthday to surround herself with friends and celebrate herself at her ranch in London, Texas. So, she takes me home with her. These trips for her have become ritualized over time. If she goes home through Dallas, she stops to eat at the Highland Park Cafeteria. If she goes through San Antonio, she stops to eat at Luby's Cafeteria. We go through San Antonio, she rents a car, we drive by the River Walk, she points out the Alamo, and we go to eat at Luby's. She craves the fried okra and banana cream pie. She has eight "side" dishes, no entree. Four of the eight are desserts. I have two entrees, two side dishes, refills of iced tea. No desserts. We are different this way. She has a sweet tooth for Texas.

We begin the four-hour drive from San Antonio to London through the Hill Country, and the more we get away from the big city, the more she relaxes. Her body relaxes, she stops smoking as often, she fiddles with the radio stations to find the most "country" she can find. She explains to me that she comes down here every April, just to see the bluebonnets and Indian paintbrush, all the wildflowers that populate the hillsides like so many lush exotic pimples. But in September the hills are parched and brown with sunburning, sleepy and bald. There are walnut trees, cedars, live oak, and mesquite. There are stunted pecan trees and matted chalky trees, trees full of coiled cobwebs and old nests that look to me like shrunken heads from some old primeval voodoo rites that were poorly attended and, so, discontinued.

There are few cars on the rippled roads, each crest of a hill revealing a new postcard shot for a camera, all land, few animals, no people, and I am wondering to myself, Where are all the world's homeless? Gail drives eighty and more. She knows when to gun and when to slow down. I see little ladders from time to time, leaning at a slant to the range fences. She tells me these are stiles, and they used to be there for tourists, in lieu of portapots or outhouses, until the ranchers got tired of strangers defecating on their land. Occasionally, tourists try them, at the risk of sudden discovery and buckshot.

The hills wreak havoc with the radio, and we are constantly shifting stations. These Hill Country stations play none of the Nashville names and few of the more famous Texan singers like Willie Nelson, Waylon Jennings, or Jerry Jeff Walker. They have their own brand of country: more fiddle and faster, more whine and twang to the singer's voice, simpler songs about sorry loves and bouncing babies off a knee, no references to the world outside.

We stop for gas and a sandwich. The bread is a pretext to this sandwich, soppy with barbecue sauce. The meat is beef or pork, smoked and strong. The store people treat Gail with respect. She speaks to them in a lilting drawl, not smiling exactly, but as though she were smiling. Up north I would find this voice of hers a bit on the sweet side, syrupy, somehow insincere, as though she were buttering these people, softening up their hard edges, taming them. Down here the voice is natural, echoed in the store people's lilt and politeness, yes sir and yes ma'am courtesies exchanged like dance cards in days of yore.

We move on, and I wonder what she is thinking, but she doesn't seem to be thinking at all. She seems to be rather in a driving reverie, a slow recapture of lost memories and landscapes. In a small town we go through, she points out the Sunday houses, these little one-room huts where the cowboys and farmers used to come, before or after church, to change out of riding clothes or farm clothes and into church finery, to take a rest before the long horseride back to a ranch or farm that might have been twenty or thirty miles away. The cowboys are long gone, but the Sunday houses are still there as reminders, metonymies of absence, mausoleums without the bodies. They didn't make it into Larry McMurtry's novels or James Michener's Texas book. I heard the first lines to a poem once that said something like: "Haven't seen any people yet, but the scarecrows are crooked." The Sunday houses affect me like the lines of the poem: I haven't seen many of the people yet, but I've seen the Sunday houses, and they have weathered well, they have survived all the abandonment of Indians and Texas Rangers, the Civil War and the lure of big cities. I like the propriety they stood for, the break in the action they gave. One-man motels, not much bigger than Catholic confessional boxes.

I haven't seen a cactus yet. My stereotype of Texas has lots of cactus plants. Maybe much of what I do see belongs to the cactus family, and I don't recognize it as such. I think of what I am to this landscape. I am a what? A rube, a dude, a city slicker, a no-account Yankee. There are probably more colorful names I'll never know about.

I drive for a spell. I notice that the speed limit signs list three different speeds: fifty-five, sixty, and sixty-five. I know that one is for daytime, another for night, and I don't understand the third. Maybe it's for trucks. I drive on. Gail operates the stations on the radio, lights the cigarettes, points out the occasional opossum, squirrel, cattle, horses, even deer. I look or don't look, but always I nod my head. The driver occupies the silent seat. When Gail was driving, I entertained her with talk, questions, games. Now it is her turn to emcee and my turn to listen, nod, relax.

A police car going in the opposite direction makes a dramatic U-turn and comes up behind us, his lights flashing. I look at the speedometer as I brake. I am going seventy. He tells me I was doing seventy-five, he has clocked me doing seventy-five on his radar, I am to get out and join him in his car. I sit on the passenger side, while he writes up a ticket. He seems delighted that I am from somewhere else.

"Cold up there right now, I expect."

"Yes sir," I say. I have decided to be polite.

He begins talking about a Cajun restaurant up the road.

"It's mighty good food," he says, "although the prices are kinda gamey."

He looks at me, perhaps to see if I can afford gamey prices.

Gail gets out of the rental car, stands by the door, looking at us.

"I guess you'll be hearing about this," he says, looking at Gail.

"I don't know what you mean," I say. Then I add, "sir."

"She looks like she might be the one to wear the pants," he says, smiling. "That's all I meant."

I want to tell him it's none of his damn business, that he has no right to make personal comments about either one of us, that the extent of his authority over us is to write a ticket or not. Period. But I don't say so.

He finishes the ticket and hands me a copy. I have choices: show up in court three weeks hence, get a lawyer and fight the ticket, or mail in my guilty plea with a check.

"So, what do you think of our Texas hospitality now?" he says, showing me nicotine-stained teeth.

I feel baited, goaded, powerless to play this game, absolutely without rights to speak. I think to myself that such badgering would never take place with a fellow Texan, but I can't be completely sure.

"I hadn't noticed any," I say, getting out of the car.

Small revenge. Gail has already resumed her place at the wheel. I get in, and we wait until the cop makes another U-turn and continues in the opposite direction. I am angry as I tell her what has happened in the cop's car. I expect her to be angry too, but she just laughs. She thinks the hospitality question is very funny. I pout. After she has stopped amusing herself with the incident, she speaks to me.

"Everybody gets speeding tickets in Texas. Don't take it so personally."

It takes me another twenty miles to let go of it and forget about whether I will pay the ticket or not. We get to Fredericksburg, which is one of Gail's most favorite places in the whole world. This is not just a ten-minute stop. She tells me we will be here for several hours, while she walks up one side of the street and down the other, poking her head in every single shop. Her favorite place is the German bakery, where she buys herself three cream puffs and a bottled Coca Cola. She buys a bushel of peaches that look small to me and overripe, but these peaches are the snack foods for the ranch. She buys jewelry here, some good-luck amulet made by Indians, always in the form of little animals. She tells me she still has the amulets she bought here when she was in high school. I buy a pair of Rocky walking shoes and make the mistake of stopping in the other bakery in town. This is heresy, of course, for to Gail there is only one bakery worth going to, and it's the other one.

Fredericksburg is full of patchwork quilts and funny store signs that say "Das Shoppe" or "Das Peach Haus" or some such Germanized English for tourists. The town is full of tourists, all looking for approximately the same things, all making the same rounds, a kind of unspoken queue up and down the main street. It reminds me of tourists among the Amish back home in Pennsylvania or tourists at Main Street, USA, in Magic Kingdom at Disney World. To me, the town is full of simulacra, the tourist industry seems to be the only industry, it's hard to tell what is authentically Fredericksburg, what is "native" and what is facade, and, besides, the prices are kinda gamey. But to Gail Fredericksburg represents countless stops with her grandmother when she was a child, on their way to San Antonio and back, and she laps up the nostalgia with every step she takes. When she is eating cream puffs, stuffing herself beyond what hunger would ever require, she is eating memories, the smells of this town, the safety she felt as a little girl. I understand all of this finally and do not pout or present myself as the impatient escort. I give myself over to the three hours it takes us to get on the road again. Besides, Fredericksburg is full of Sunday houses, so my patience is rewarded.

When we drive off, I am really eager to get to the ranch, while she is sated, sleepy, becalmed, much as I imagine Mexicans after hours at the *mercado* look to siesta. The rest of the drive takes us through Mason, where we must stop again, because now we need bottled water, milk, eggs, and other perishables for the ranch. We stop, stock up on groceries, and drive again.

The rest of the way begins to feel like her landscape. The side roads are not as well kept, the hills are more idiosyncratic and less "scenic," and the whole place begins to feel wilder, more primitive. We have to watch out for deer or cattle in the road. We can't find a radio station any longer. We pass by small places with signs and a cemetery: sign and a cemetery, nothing more.

"Streeter."

"Long Mountain."

"Little Saline."

"Grit."

Gail tells me that all of these used to be towns, or at least town-lets, hamlets before the war, and that they collapsed, disappeared, their survivors moving off to bigger towns or even cities as the economy shifted, leaving only the dead behind, the tombstones as testimonials of family dead.

"I keep meaning to ask my father about these places," she says, "but I never have."

They catch your eye, you want to know more, but you drive on, get distracted, and never ask. You're always moving when you see them, and so you forget to ask about them, because such moving things have trouble standing still in memory long enough to be asked about. These cemetery towns are like subliminal ads for a Texas that once was. They are arguably more dramatic and more poignant than the Sunday houses, but somehow they don't stick like the Sunday houses.

I think it odd and somehow poetic. Up north, at least in my native Michigan, you would never find a sign-and-cemetery seclusion. The dead themselves have no need of the grounds in which they're buried, no proprietary sense of their own enshrinement, and so cemeteries must be for the living to continue the dead. If there's a cemetery, it means there must be *living* people nearby. But land up north is less land, more at a premium, and so cemeteries are sometimes dug up, rototilled, given over to something else, like a school or shopping mall. Here in Texas there is land enough to include the bygone as well as the ongoing. I am touched as we pass "Grit" to note that there are fresh flowers next to one of the stones, but the stone itself is so weathered by time that I can't read the name. Maybe only the person who brought the flowers knows that name anymore. Gail nods. She's silent behind the steering wheel, but I can see she likes this thought of mine, even though I'm not totally sure I ever expressed it aloud.

We turn off just before the town of London and drive the dirt road to her ranch. Twenty minutes of wretched road, full of big rocks, fallen trees, and deep cracks and gullies, driving at no more than ten miles per hour. We get to her gate and I think we are there, but no. Nothing has prepared me for this. I am thinking of the ranches on *Dallas*, the sedate sprawls. But this ranch is twenty times the scope of those TV ranches. This ranch is wild, primitive, not meant for cars to travel, almost not meant for people. I count five more gates that we pass through. Gail calls them bump gates. She accelerates, hits them squarely with the grill of the car, they open, we pass through, they close behind us. These gates not only separate the various pastures, one from another, but they also keep the stock from wandering off. If there is a cow in the road, we wait until it moves. Horses, deer, even occasional goats, it's the same protocol of wait or drive around. Trees grow every which way along the stony road, the casualties of time and storms. Stones carom off the car's axle, and the sound scares away some of the cows, who move in slow motion when they move at all. I can hear wild sounds: crickets in the cool evening air, frogs, sometimes a hissing that I think must be snakes. There are prickly cactus plants for miles around, pea-soup green and bloated with liquid. The ground between them looks gouged and brown, the aftermath of summer, when it had the color and texture of a pool table carpet.

The road enlarges and becomes almost driveworthy, which is to say, almost fit for humans, just before we get to the ranch house. I can hear water from a steep decline behind the cabin. The Llano River runs through her property, and she has water rights. This ranch and the land around it, at least the half dozen pastures around it, belong to her now, all hers. She alone, the librarian from up north, kept the land and didn't sell. There is something like the look new mothers have, looking at their babies, in Gail's eyes as she parks the car and looks around. It's not the ranch house she cares about, not the hunting, fishing, or swimming, nothing civilized or having to do with sports or rules. It's the wild itself she cares about, the way you have to leave ownership and anthropomorphism outside the outermost gate, the way you have to come in wide eyed and quiet, sharing the time and the land with the grown stock and wild animals, mindful of the Indians who once roamed these mountains, moving from one night fire to another.

The librarian in Gail is gone now, replaced by what? By some kind of frontierswoman, mix of awe and respect in her eyes, anxious to discover, but careful not to disturb, the ecology of the place. It's as though she's wandered into someone else's national park site instead of her own property.

"Don't turn the porch light on just yet," she says as I am opening the door, my arms full of grocery bags. "We might hear the deer crossing."

Every night under the moon whole families of deer run across the Llano where the river is at its shallowest, making splash-paddle sounds in the water, then clacking like the hooves of horses when they reach the long, flat rocks, where the river rises and sometimes floods after heavy rains, then sinks and exposes the rocks again in dry times.

I expect mosquitoes or other evening bugs, but there aren't any. I hear fish breaking water farther downstream where it's deeper. The moon is out, and it looks as though it never gets any darker than this lazy blue, so that one could stay out all night on the flat rocks and see for miles, at least skyward. I don't know whether to speak or be quiet. I decide to pretend I'm driving, I'm the one behind the wheel, so all I have to do is nod, listen, and be still until spoken to. Sure enough, finally the deer do cross, and it's an eerie sight, their antlers glistening in the moonlight. They are most visible at the top, most audible at the bottom. They bunch together and look skittish, afraid, ready to spray out in four directions if given cause. For some reason, I think of Indians, a war party out for a night foray, their jagged feathers giving them away in the moonbeams. Once the deer leave the rocks for the upward climb through angled trees and stones, I can't see them anymore. I can only hear twigs break, stones scatter, like a gravel road's pandemonium. They have scared a rabbit or two, whose bodies we recognize only by the white ruff of their tails.

Gail gives off a deep sigh, as though this sight alone were performed for our benefit and worth the entire trip, and she says we can go in now. Going inside might be what most people would do first. You unpack the car, put away the perishables, survey the beds and dressers, have a drink, then maybe you walk outside. It is clear to me that Gail admires the animals who don't go in anywhere and that going inside is somehow a statement of defeat, an acknowledgment of our weakness as people.

There is a satellite dish at the ranch, installed so that her brothers can get any sports event they want at any given time. More than nine bands and two hundred channels to choose from. I get a Spanish station from South America, a French station out of Montreal. The television brings the global village to this ranch outside London, Texas. Gail doesn't use it.

Her father built this particular bunkhouse, then billed her for it. The former ranch house, the one she grew up in, still stands downstream on land now owned by someone else. Gail has disdain for this more modern version, with its two complete bedrooms and six extra cots, its restaurant-sized black grill for frying steaks, its laundry room. The touches are all her father's. Gail seems to ascribe to the line from Willie Nelson in the film *Barbarosa:* "What cannot be changed must be endured." She endures the new cabin, but she will not take joy from it.

She much prefers the "hunter's cabin," a shack of a house right on the river, where Mexican friends of the foreman sometimes stay. She says she will fix it up one day. It's not the insides that attract her as much as the wooden deck, the place where the Llano runs stereo through both ears, the proximity to the water and deer, to the mountains in the distance.

She knows the pastures by heart, and we go by jeep to her favorite pasture, some four miles away from the cabin, the one that contains Geronimo's Cave. Legend has it that Geronimo actually hid out in this cave once upon a time. But then legend has a lot of things. Jim Bowie may have buried his silver mine in one of these mountains. Nobody has ever found the treasure, but it hasn't been for want of looking. I remember the famous line spoken by the newspaper reporter to Jimmy Stewart in *The Man Who Shot Liberty Valence:* "Senator, when the legend is larger than the truth in the Old West, we print the legend." What is true here is that the real thing is spectacular enough to encourage the legend. I have fanny fatigue from the jeep ride, one in which our bodies have been lifted off the seats and slammed down again by the many rocks, more so, I think, than if we had ridden bucking broncos in a rodeo.

At Geronimo's Cave, the river is placid, almost a still life. Soft tinted grass, green and brown, grows by the banks, giving the impression of a nurtured place, a cozy grove, a picnic site. The "wilds" are all on the other side in the form of the cave we don't go to but only stare at and wonder. I see a goat come out of the mouth of the cave. I see an eagle fly overhead. Gail spots an armadillo on our side, and we give quiet chase for a while. We don't think to swim here, fish here, or otherwise "work" the landscape. This vista is just for looking. I ask her how it feels to own such a place, and she answers that such places cannot be owned; they were here before she came along and they will be here after she's gone. I understand how a little girl who grew up with this as her "special" place might not be very awed by the Pyramids, the Eiffel Tower, or anywhere else on earth. You don't replace such a space as a grown-up. I realize that I have never been in a place where I could scream at the top of my lungs and have no one hear. This place boggles me, my sense of "neighborhood." In my wildest cowboy fantasies as a boy, I never envisioned such a place.

The "tourism" of the jeep ride back includes mean wild horses that will kick you if you get too close, more deer, some brooding cattle, and the shed skin of a rattlesnake. She says in the summer there are a lot of water moccasins in the river and you have to be careful where you swim and how you swim. We stop for her to check the deer feeder, we look out at all the prickly cactus, the live oak trees, wild berries, the good smell of unlaundered land and the gamy smells of animals that have never been tamed. I wonder, if we stayed here long enough, would we begin to smell like that: feral, unkempt, full of our surroundings and the wild things we ate? It occurs to me that the old cave dwellers didn't brush their teeth, wear deodorant, wash themselves regularly, so they probably did smell like the pelts and hides they wore, the gristle of meat dried on their fingers like a paste. And now that Geronimo and his band are gone, we have only occasional glimpses into such primitive smells.

We go back to the cabin to wash up and head out to the London Dance Hall. It's Saturday night, and there's always a dance at the London Dance Hall. Gail wears something like a cowgirl outfit, studded replicas of the state of Texas on her vest, sleek jeans, and boots. I laugh to myself and begin to wonder if every woman there is going to look like Dale Evans. I think I must look out of place, of course, because I have nothing Texan on, and even if I did, I wouldn't fool anyone.

Once again, my expectations are worlds apart from the reality. I expect a gaudy place, some sort of silver palace with lots of mirrors behind the bar and glittering floors. I expect a lot of good ole boys getting drunk and rowdy, till they have to go outside for fistfights. I expect to be able to tell the difference between the farmers and ranchers, the townspeople and tourists. What I find instead is something like an oversized barn, drab in decor, nothing fancy about the walls or floors or bathrooms. Everything has been sacrificed for dancing, all the tables arranged around the walls and the vast open middle for couples. Some of the best bands in Texas come to play here, and, instrumental or voiced, the music has a sameness to it, at least to my ears, more fiddle than guitar, more voice than drums, and all the music conducive to the Texas two-step or some variation on it. There are entire families here, and everyone dances: moms and pops, sisters and brothers, grandparents and little children. There is a smooth traffic flow to the couples, the men stiff from the belt up, agile from the stomach down, shuffling their boots, and the women moving backward, never a looking around or sense of vertigo. Everyone drinks bottled beer at the tables, and there is lots of loud talking and laughter, but no rowdy cowboys, as far as I can tell.

I am impressed that whole families dance together, that children are in this smoke-filled place and enjoying themselves, and that, finally, everybody dances with everybody else, with very short breaks between the songs. It takes the band a song or two to introduce themselves, and by then nobody is listening anyway. Gail dances nonstop. I sit and watch, nurse my beer, sit and watch. She comes back between dances to check on me, then goes off again.

I stare at feet, the hundred pairs of feet, trying to memorize the steps and imagine myself doing them. Finally, I try, but I either lose the beat or get crossed up with my feet. I can't turn corners. I push my partner into other couples. I am a disaster, so I beg to sit down again, and she agrees. Maybe there's a hotbed of sin here, marriages making it or breaking it over the beer and the two-step, but I am unaware of it. I think the whole thing is wholesome, graceful, and I know of nothing quite like it back home. Maybe square dances and clogging groups. Maybe the classes my mother made me take at the Arthur Murray studios when I was a boy, so I could learn to polka and foxtrot, dances that did me no good in the folksinging or rock-and-roll sixties.

Gail loves to dance here, and it's not the partner that counts, although a good partner is a plus, or the music, the beers, the smoke in the air like a fog. It's the dancing itself, the free feel of the feet back home on native soil, the mixing with strangers who are her people, dancing to music that hasn't much changed since she was ten. And maybe, I think to myself, this is the anti-dote for loneliness, the corrective for all the harshly beautiful and impersonal terrain, this coming together on Saturday nights, this nameless commingling, this orderly procession of couples going round and round.

Up north we might sit together, people-watch, and pass summary judgments on the couples. Isn't he ugly? That one looks mean. She's decked out. Look at the jewels on that one. Here everyone fits; there is no one who is ugly, too old to dance, too young to dance. The best dancers are often some of the older couples, years of marriage and years of dancing conspiring to make their movements so graceful and synchronized.

"So, how do you like our Texas hospitality now?" she asks me suddenly, pinching me out of my meditations.

There is not so much a late and a later here, where people leave little by little. Instead, there's closing time, "last call," the last song of the last band, and everyone leaves at once. We go back to the ranch in the jeep, which is a real adventure by moonlight. The wind blows a brisk, cold four-arm shiver against my face. My eyes water to be outside and away from all the smoke. My mouth is open and dry from wind. Gail drives, and we bounce from one crevice to another, off one rock exploding against the axle to another. The jeep is better on the bump gates than a rental car, and Gail accelerates with confidence. I see constant darting off to the sides of the headlight beams: rabbits, squirrels, opossums, all lookalikes by speed, low and fleet and from the rodent family.

I know better than to go inside immediately. We go down to the flat rocks, still warm from the day's heat. We lie down. My feet hurt, not because I have danced often or well, but because I have been outdoors and on the go in a strange place all day. I look up at the sky and recognize only Orion among the thousands of stars. Gail still sits, waiting to see the deer cross. She looks pleased, sated, a little high. I think about those beer commercials where the men sit around the campfire eating the bass they've caught, and somebody inevitably says, "It doesn't get any better than this." I can imagine a film crew, low angle up, capturing us in the moonlight as the deer cross the river, our faces flushed with beer, dancing, and a windy drive in the jeep, and I get to say, "It doesn't get any better than this." But who knows? Maybe it does. I have been wrong a dozen times since arriving in Texas.

The friendship is twenty-two years old. It seems like five the last time we marked it. We don't sleep together, Gail and I, even though the love between us is deep, the sexual attraction is there, and various hand holding, hugging, and kissing over the years would suggest that the lovemaking would be good. We're both afraid of tampering with the friendship, somehow altering it or losing it. It's a sign of aging, we both think, that we have come to value the rarity of a best friend over the possibility of being lovers.

In time the friends and family show up to celebrate her birthday. Mimi, her former roommate, comes from Boston by way of a business meeting in Paris. Truman, her brother-in-law, comes from San Antonio. Bobby, Ruthie, and another Gail, old college friends, come from Dallas. Her brother Craig comes with his girlfriend and his children, Krystal and Josh. Her father comes with another couple, friends of his. Her favorite uncle and aunt come from San Angelo. Others will show up and leave during the weekend. There are ten cars parked outside.

Suddenly, there is noise everywhere. The television is on non-stop, turned from one ball game to another. Men sit together and smoke cigars. The women sit in the kitchen or at the eating table, preparing food or playing cards with the children. Everyone has a bottle of beer. The making of meals for so many people becomes a monumental task of several hours. The cleaning up leads right into the preparations for the next meal. The smells of breakfast eggs and sausage still permeate the kitchen when lunch is being prepared. People escape by twos and threes for a walk on the river, a ride in the jeep to Geronimo's Cave, some rifle shooting out back, fishing downstream where the bass are. We rarely notice who is gone, because there are still so many left.

I notice this behavior in my friend Gail. She gives complete respect and deference to her Uncle Walter and Aunt Dora for the time that they are there. They are given center stage and treated like the guests of honor. She pulls out a cake she bought at the bakery in Fredericksburg and celebrates her father's birthday, which is two days after her birthday, instead of celebrating her own. She gives thus to her father and to the children, Krystal and Josh, for children in her hierarchy are always guests of honor too. Mimi, Guy, Truman, and I are asked to help, to go talk to her father when she can't. It's a form of Zen, I think, that those she sees least should get the most attention and those she knows the best should be overlooked and counted upon to stand in for her as co-hosts. This respect for elders and doting on children seems more Japanese or Chinese to me than American, but I know this is her hierarchy, she is loyal to that hierarchy, and I am loyal to her. So I wash dishes, take the kids for a ride in the jeep, talk to her father and uncle, because to do otherwise would be rude, and rudeness is a capital sin in Gail's world. That and verbal insults, which she suffers less than injurious acts. What is said is more harmful in her eyes than what is done. The librarian in her, I think.

I like the way that Texans with names in the diminutive stay that way all their lives. Bobby is around the same age as Gail, old enough to be Bob or Robert, but he will always be Bobby and Ruthie will never be Ruth. I remember being Billy for a time when I was young, Billy to my friends and my parents. If I had grown up in Texas, I would still be Billy. And Gail has a way of going formal sometimes, when she says "shan't" and "perchance" and calls me William. It doesn't mean she feels an emotional distance. It just means the topic at hand seems to require it. I am suddenly William when she is asking me for a ride to the airport or talking to me about my weight or lecturing me on the evils of fried foods. I am Bill again when I make her laugh, when we're watching a movie or shopping at a mall. I have been Bill when we watched the deer cross and went to the London Dance Hall, but now that her father and uncle and other friends are around, I am occasionally William again. Nobody else has ever called me William, so I don't mind.

I take photographs for the occasion. Gail, her brother, and her father *do* look alike, even if they wear on each other like birch trees in the same cluster. They have the same piercing eyes, unblinking eyes, eagle stares. They have the same thin lips, often pursed like a taunt, the same strong chins, the same loud horse-drawn laughter. Craig's children look the opposite, more Indian than Germanic, dark and olive skinned, with soft eyes and big flashy smiles. Gail's skin looks bleached next to Krystal's. Krystal has a way of describing everything as "big ole": the big ole tree, the big ole bear in her storybook, the big ole deer she saw outside. At ten, she is completely charming, already spoiled for life by her striking good looks, a femme fatale in the making. Josh is a sports nut, a clone of his father. Craig is holding court for the grown-ups, telling jokes, relating the horror stories of the commodities market. He tells us he wants to see a game in Yankee Stadium and one in Fenway Park before he dies. Apparently, he has already made his pilgrimage to Wrigley Field and other romantic old ballparks. He, too, is charming. I look around me. Everyone is talking, laughing and talking, everyone is "hosting," and there are precious few listeners to go around. What few there are, are women.

What is true at the ranch in Texas, and I imagine it has been true of ranches in Texas for over one hundred years, is that no matter how late you stay up, you still get up when the sun gets up. There are no drapes on the windows to keep out the sun. People get up, their minds get up, even though they may be bone weary and blurred of vision. Gail puts on CDs of Edith Piaf to help the wake-up process along. The smell of breakfast eggs and meats cuts right through sleep. I get up to go to the bathroom, whose floor is already wet from several showers that have preceded me. Gail goes without sleep two nights in a row, laughing and entertaining the night owls among her guests. She looks haggard, drawn, the color gone from her face.

The weekend finally ends by Sunday afternoon, a brilliant painter's palette of a day whose light hurts the eyes of those who lack sleep, and everyone goes home but the hard-core inner circle. There is much work to do: beds to be made, floors to be swept and mopped, trash to be burned, food to be packed or given away to the animals and birds. No one is hungry. I feel bloated from so much protein and starch. I give my gifts to Gail, who is happy to be remembered, but yawning freely now, letting herself let down at last. Truman drinks the last beer and says we need the stimulus of a drive in an "assault vehicle" to a good shopping mall. Mimi, who has worked like a maid for three days, plays solitaire, withdraws, won't answer when we speak to her. Guy, who has been telling jokes all weekend, goes from cot to cot, trying to get sleep. We're all that tired, barely able to keep going. None of us wants the day to end, but we're all on the edge of being antisocial from too many people, too much politeness, too much fatigue.

I look at Gail and think I see Barbara Stanwyck, she of all those westerns in which she ran the ranch by herself, in lieu of a husband or foreman. The strength of Barbara Stanwyck's face is there, the stubborn determination, the will to power, the haughty bloodlines and finesse that transcend the management of a ranch. I still see the librarian in her, she who reads four or five books a week, who tells stories like a professional, the master programmer who matches the library's resources with the community's needs, she who has given her entire working life to the cause of literacy. There are no libraries at the ranch, in London, or anywhere else nearby. Yet now I cannot imagine her without this ranch, even the absentee ownership of it. Like Antaeus touching the earth, this ranch is both her getaway place and her energy source.

I know there are poor people in Texas. I cannot speak to them. There are personality profiles that could be drawn from Houston, Austin, Corpus Christi, and El Paso. I cannot speak to them. Clearly, Gail was born to privilege, reasonable wealth, people of means. She did not go wanting in her childhood, and she does not lack for material comforts now. Still, she has suffered, from patriarchal neglect and old sores that never healed. She has been warped by her upbringing, skewed by her source, formed and hardened and petrified by her past. And since she has paid her considerable dues, I do not see her simply as a working woman from Philadelphia who magically transforms into a wealthy woman in Texas. I see her as *natural* to this place, this place as natural to her.

I have learned a lot about Texas and her in Texas in a short time. Perhaps too much. Sometimes, those who work from stereotypes get to some partial truths more directly than those who do their research in the field and thereby complicate their judgments. Gail and I still share this twinship, this fellow feeling of same prejudices, common feelings, similar values, and a mutual ESP of interactive health, moods, and mind-sets, but now I don't know where it comes from. I have nothing in my past to compare with her Texas. I have been initially overwhelmed by almost everything I have seen, and then I have seen my spirit soar to encompass the terrain or the terrain shrink from repeated vision to the size of my eyes, the way big meals and small meals are relative and sometimes interchangeable. We go back to Philadelphia, and the city seems bleak, desultory, overcrowded, badly planned, poorly nourished, a nightmare of too many people thrown together in too small a place. I miss the special obsession of a memory bakery, the sign and cemetery of a time gone by, the nighttime streaking of startled deer. The lore of the Liberty Bell seems stoical and rote remembered when compared with the folklore of the Alamo, its ongoing mix of truth and tall tales. I can't reproduce the good feelings of the ranch by suddenly walking with a saddle-vee swagger, wearing plaid shirts with pearlized snaps, or saying "gol-lee" in response to everything I hear. Texans, it seems to me, can more easily go abroad and steal a Broadway show, the cherry blossoms of a D.C. spring, the slopes of Snowbird, Vail, or Aspen, even a third-base box seat in Fenway Park, than the rest of us can go and steal anything away from Texas. Maybe this is the majesty of that state after all: it sneaks inside your skin, it gets you to longing and pining away, but it resists looting. You have to go back for the bluebonnets and Indian paintbrush; they won't come to your neighborhood lawn party.

Gail calls me William when she says we will retire one day to "pasture-sit." Prior to my trip to Texas, pasture-sitting sounded like scarecrows in a cornfield, like birds that don't sow or toil in the lilies of the field. Now I understand those pastures to be alive with animals who smell fierce with untaming and sitting to be anything but sedentary. When I factor in occasional forays into civilization for cream puffs, peaches, and dancing, it's not a half-bad retirement dream. The way Bogart and Claude Rains walk off into the unknown at the end of *Casablanca* is similar to the way I sometimes see Gail and me jeeping off to Geronimo's Cave for a picnic and a powwow with invisible Apaches. No deadlines to meet, no return date to anywhere, no limit on the hospitality.

P.S.: I paid the speeding ticket.

Homes of Memory Glue

Maybe Mister Rogers makes us think about our neighborhoods. But even his neighborhood, the focal point for me being the closet where he hangs his sweater and keeps his sneakers, has the "escape" valve of the Land of Make-Believe. Few of us think about our neighborhoods beyond the impact of the seasons in our own backyards: there's snow, there are leaves to rake, there's lawn to water. Some of us have gone back to the small towns we grew up in, to revisit the house we used to live in, the neighborhood we used to roam. And maybe the houses have not aged well. Maybe they seem small to us now, so small we can't imagine how big they used to feel when we were little. And perhaps the neighborhood has fallen into disrepair, time and suburbs and shopping malls have passed it by, the houses all look spectral, ghost houses that seem to be crying out for former owners, younger bodies, better times. My parents were people who thought about moving every two years or so, but they never did; instead, they built on: a longer porch, a back bedroom, a family room where the peach tree and cherry tree used to be. The result was a sprawling house that took up the better part of two lots, with no apparent architectural style at all, except perhaps some of the funny polygons from German expressionism and a film like *The Cabinet of Doctor Caligari.* So now my own ancestral home in Michigan, which raised seven children, has been bought and sold several times since my father sold it. Currently, it's a fraternity house for the local college. Last year, my sister and I begged a tour of the inside, and the boys of Beta House agreed to let us in. There was a water bed in every bedroom, a paddle with the Beta logo on every door, photographs of girlfriends on nightstands. We had walked into an archaeological "dig" of our own undoing. Hard to tell a family of seven children had lived there for twenty-some years. It was an interesting experience, a sobering experience, sad and provocative both. I wager that few people would want to drag their childhood memories through such a shock chamber of change. A simple drive-by might have done just as well. You keep the outside neutral that way and save the inside in your mind, a mausoleum of no changes.

In nearby Essexville my grandmother and grandfather used to run a hotel/rooming house. When I was very little, it was a rooming house, my grandparents living on the ground floor and seven or eight other tenants occupying the second and third floors. At some point, though, it was more officially known as a hotel. That may have been after my grandfather died and my grandmother came to live with us. Rooming house or hotel, my grandmother ran it, while my grandfather went to work on the day shift at General Motors. I had just as keen an interest in revisiting that neighborhood, one in which my grandmother also was the first official Spic and Span distributor and the unofficial midwife for over two hundred births, as I had in seeing the house of my father and mother. But my sons were only interested in the latter, not at all in the former. The house of my grandparents was too remote, too many generations removed, for my sons to care about.

Maybe the curiosity of memory only extends as far as two generations, the personal relationships my sons have with their parents and grandparents. To be curious further back than that seems to imply a shift from personal memory to history itself, the kind of shift that growing up and aging make possible. And one side of the family usually takes precedence over the other, like dominant and recessive traits in gene charting. My father is the only grandparent still alive on my side of the family, and we know that he came from a farm outside Bay City, but we have never bothered to find that farm. In our culture in general and in my own experience in particular, the mother marked the home, not only with all her influence, but with all her relatives as well. Fathers may dominate in the workplace, in earning power and the continuation of family name, but they tend to be recessive in terms of family trees.

My point here is less one of genealogy, however, than of geography. The neighborhood in which we raise our children, whether it has ever counted as spiritual "home" to us or not, is the neighborhood of record, the geography of memories. And this neighborhood is itself a stand-in, an extended family tree of trees, a mapping of the territory we call memory.

This mapping is often drawn quixotically, idiosyncratically, without apparent regard for logic or pattern or balance. For example, the bathroom in my grandparents' rooming house in Essexville had a clothes chute that went to a big straw basket in the basement. I used to pitch my grandfather's hairbrush, toothbrush, razors, and cologne, his entire toilette, down that clothes chute, which sometimes made him late for work in the morning and for which I incurred his wrath in spiteful French Canadian, but my grandmother always protected me, made him go to the basement to fetch his things and scolded him for cussing out a child. From the clothes chute, which was more the focal point of that house for me than the fireplace or kitchen, I "graduated" to the various sewers outside, places from which my grandfather could never retrieve his things. And one day my grandmother tossed my teddy bear down the clothes chute, unbeknownst to me of course, and she made me pray to Saint Anthony for its safe return. I dutifully got down on hands and knees and prayed to Saint Anthony, the cure-all for every lost thing. When I awoke from my afternoon nap, my teddy bear was mysteriously next to my face on the pillow. She proclaimed the miracle, and we had a celebratory supper at which my grandfather begrudgingly acknowledged the miracle too, after much scolding from my grandmother. That same week I went on my longest walk away from their house, a walk that was probably no more than eight or nine blocks, but long enough for me to realize that I was lost, did not know my way back, and was in need of another consultation with Saint Anthony. I wasn't scared. I knew getting lost was the price to pay for so much exploration, and even then, at the age of five or six, I remember thinking to myself that I was becoming a big boy now, because I had walked so far from home. Sure enough, soon a grown-up came to take me by the hand and lead me back to the rooming house, without ever asking my name or who my people were. My grandmother, as I remember it, had tears in her eyes. She looked like she might be ready to smack me, if she weren't so glad to see me again. She told me I had made her worry. I told her she needn't have worried. I prayed to Saint Anthony and was found, and I proclaimed the miracle. She agreed, although she was in no mood for a celebratory supper. From the clothes chute, I had tamed the many sewers. From the lost teddy bear, I had tamed the many sidewalks. The idiosyncratic event had served to map the larger territory, such that the cold, impersonal neighborhood was "conquered" in a personal way.

In my own neighborhood in Midland, I learned to stretch the boundaries of what was known and what was unknown through ever expanding Halloween forays, through riding bicycles with my friends, through playing football in the various streets, and through competing with rival gangs (they were benign enough in those days), sneaking into their territory, staying on the look-see for if they tried to sneak into ours. At one point, I must have been around ten then, my friends and I decided that we should explore firsthand the rooftops of every house in the neighborhood. We climbed trees and drainpipes and makeshift rope ladders and touched the chimneys of every house for four blocks around. We weren't interested in doing any mischief, in spying on the homes, or in leaving any markers that we had been there. We just wanted to be able to say we had done it. This was city climbing. If we had grown up in the jungles with Tarzan, we would have climbed baobab trees and swung from vines instead of drainpipes and shaky eaves. We understood our need to climb on this level, and it made perfect sense to us. I had my own fear of heights to contend with, a fear I never disclosed to my friends, and when I revisited the neighborhood and saw how low the rooftops were, I wondered why I had been so afraid. I have been on ski tows that went much higher up.

My children don't share these memories, and conversely I don't have their memories of this neighborhood in Philadelphia, this section of the city called Mount Airy in which we have lived for over fifteen years. I came here from graduate school when I was still married and before the children were born to take a teaching job in the city. This is the only neighborhood my sons have ever known. Many things—the collapse of the marriage, my single-parenting, my limited teacher's salary, and the skyrocketing housing market—have conspired to keep us here. This place, pretty enough with its cobblestone streets and many row homes, its Dutch elms and Japanese maples, its middle-class feel and transient shops, has never been *home* for me. I stay here for the job I have, not because the place speaks in any way to my heart, my mind, my memories. I have been here long enough to know this place will never be home to me. We live in an apartment that seems to shrink as the boys get older and bigger. I live here, but I don't *come from here*. My sons come from here, they count more in the census than I do, this place is home to them, and their memories have mapped out the territory in ways unknown or foreign to me.

I took stock the other day, a transitional day when it should still have been wintry cold but was inexplicably sunny and mild instead, just the right kind of day for reveries and taking stock. I set myself this task: to try to remember what stores preceded the stores we now have, going back fifteen years; what people used to live in the houses across the street before the people who now live there, going back fifteen years; how the nearby train station and models of cars and garden flowers used to look back then. This exercise was easier said than done, much harder, say, than answering *Trivial Pursuit* questions, and required a physical cooperation, a body stillness to open up memories.

I remember the train station when I first came here as a viable, functioning station: you could go inside, buy a ticket, have a coffee, and wait in relative warmth for your train. Flowers were planted by community civic groups like West Mount Airy Neighbors. An old man named Bob lived upstairs in the station with his dogs. He lived there rent free, a result of some forty years as an employee of Septa and Amtrak, and he was the best deterrent to crime any neighborhood could ever ask for. He was a friend to all the cops. He served them hot coffee at all hours during the night, and they patrolled the neighborhood freely and often. Now Bob has broken his hip and is in a home somewhere. The train station is closed, so commuters have to wait outside in the cold for their trains and buy their tickets on the train at full price. Bob's dogs roam the neighborhood unleashed and without an owner, dependent upon the mercy of strangers for food and water. There is graffiti everywhere on the train station walls, and now something called Town Watch, individual home owners and apartment dwellers who take turns walking the blocks with flashlights, serves as the deterrent to crime. No more manicured flower beds, no hot coffee while waiting, no patrolling police cars.

Speaking of patrolling, I remember there used to be a rather well-dressed bum who patrolled our street when I first moved here. He always wore a suit and tie, but the suit was wrinkled, the white shirt dirty, and he wore untied high-top sneakers for shoes. His hair was never combed, his face never shaven, and he had wild eyes up close, making furtive gestures toward a futile escape whenever anyone approached. I first noticed him circling my car, a blue Ambassador (before the Ford Falcon, Renault, Citation, Escort, and Camry that followed). Circling was suspicious enough, but when he put his face up to the window of the driver-side door, when he physically touched my car that way, I called the police. They came right away in those days. The cop told me he was harmless, he was merely trying to get an odometer reading for his notebook. I watched the man closely after that. He kept a book on all the cars on our street, took notes daily in a ringbinder memo pad, noting the make of car, the mileage if possible, the license tag number, any other features that caught his fancy in a fast, impressionistic scribble. He worked hard and steadily, walking this "beat" and staying on his feet until around noon, when he would sit on the curb and pull out a wrinkled sandwich from his suit coat pocket. He worked daily, nine to five, disappeared at dark, reappeared the next morning. The cop told me he didn't have a home that anyone knew about and that he probably slept in one of the train stations. How he came by his sandwich nobody knew. How he "supported" himself nobody knew. And how he came to focus so totally on our street was also a mystery. He was an unpaid worker, and his métier was annotating parked cars. I went outside one day and approached him with a sandwich and a glass of milk. He looked away, turned his body away from me, showing me only profile, as though his invisibility had somehow been deciphered and turning this way would restore his anonymity. I told him the correct mileage on the Ambassador, and he nodded gruffly, flipping to the appropriate page in his memo pad and noting the mileage. I continued to bring him food for a while, but he never accepted. Then I switched tactics and brought him brand-new pencils for his work. I told him which cars belonged to people who actually lived on the street and which cars were transient cars, those that belonged to commuters who took the train to work. I pointed to the apartment where I lived and told him he could use the phone or bathroom any time he wanted. He never answered me, and I began to think he had lost language somewhere along the line, that speech had become too difficult for him and he had given it up. I admired him for his devotion to such meaningless work, for wearing a suit and tie when it was clear he wanted nobody to notice, for a dignity that had come undone.

Eventually, I left him alone. One day I went out to my car and noticed a piece of memo pad paper affixed to the windshield. On the paper, scrawled in pencil, the notation: A-OKAY. I guess that was his way of acknowledging me. After five years or so of taking notes, circling the car, and peering through the windows, he had communicated to me: my car passed inspection. I was touched.

I knew enough not to seek him out and acknowledge receipt of the note.

One day I realized I hadn't seen him in over two years. How that much time could have gone by without noticing I don't know. The seasons change, we stay busy with our own work, we forget to notice such things. I asked Bob at the train station about the man. Bob said he thought the man had died. That was a safe enough assumption, and probably an accurate one, but I preferred to think the man had completed his work on our block and had merely moved on to another block somewhere. In the years that followed, other crazies came and went from the landscape: the duck woman, who honked like a duck when she panhandled at the train station; the millionaire bag lady, who carried all her belongings in Hefty bags; the fake mailman, who carried wadded newspapers in his shoulder pouch. I never felt their coming or going as personally as the passing of the man who took notes on parked cars.

In memory at least, it seems to me now that there was a kind of cause and effect established over the years, that each one of these eccentrics got his or her allotted time on the street, only to be replaced by the next one. The overlay of shops up on Germantown Avenue was even more blatant in its cause and effect. For example, the corner of Germantown Avenue and Allen Lane has always been a corner for groceries: first Price's Market, then the A & P, then Super Fresh, now the convenience store called WaWa. But always, whether small family market or full-fledged chain or convenience store, the corner has been somehow "zoned" for groceries.

The middles of blocks were less predictable, but over time they began to feel like cut and paste, a map of temporality and causality, linked only by the memory of he who remembers. Johnny's Antiques gave way to Vivino's Pizzeria when Johnny died, and

Vivino's gave up pizza for arcade games and selling lottery tickets. Across the street, Miss Alex's restaurant, famous for its fresh tangy chili, gave way to a garment shop, which then went into antiques. Down the block, Moran's Salvation Army store became a Five and Dime, then split into two stores, one a smoke shop, the other a comic books store. Now there's a Video Library and a Golden Crust pizzeria. Over time, the antiques, garments, and pizzas played hopscotch along the block, disappearing and reappearing in what I would call a symptomatic capitalism. Only the post office, the barber shop, and two churches have remained the same over all that time.

It is the same with people, even though we don't normally think of people in terms of symptomatic exchange. I lost a close friend who moved away on the next block, only to gain a new good friend in the person who bought the house next door to the house of the friend who left. Some neighbors were closer friends when their children used to baby-sit my children. Now my children are older, and those former baby-sitters have grown up and gone: one to live in Israel, another to work in publishing in New York City, another to school at Yale, still another to the Peace Corps. The parents of my children's friends have become my friends. The coincidental becomes bizarre in the light of memory. The same apartment in my building housed two successive tenants who became my close friends after my marriage collapsed. It wasn't planned that way. It just happened, and the causality I now see in that strange fact is one I can only note, not explain.

All of these memories, from my point of view, are a tourist's memories. They link me to these people and this place, I am clearly part of what now seems like a chain, but there is no lien of loyalty for me.

These are not home base memories such as my children have.

I hear them reminisce with each other, remembrances not especially for my ears, and I am surprised, struck by their poignancy. They remember raiding Mrs. Davis's strawberry patch next door. I remember commiserating with Mrs. Davis for years about those missing strawberries and what kind of thief would do such a thing. The thief turns out to be my children. They remember placing fifty-cent pieces and silver dollars on the train tracks and how they appreciated the pancake-shaped elliptical mangle they got after a train had passed. I remember finding such mangled metal in the laundry downstairs, and I thought for years they were part of the washer or dryer that had broken off and mixed with my wash. They spoke of hiding in the trees and not answering when I circled the building, calling their names and wondering where they had wandered off to. They remembered shoplifting jawbreakers at the old A & P when I wasn't looking. They remembered Bob threatening to poke their eyes out if they played too close to the train station. They remembered baby-sitters sneaking beer and having parties when I was gone, calling their friends on the phone, who came over and woke up my children to wrestle with them. They remembered one of the superintendents having a gun and shooting pigeons who got too close to the dumpster at the back of the driveway. They remembered eating mud and bugs and dandelions.

These are home base memories for them. They are not my memories. If I am mentioned at all, I am only tangential to these memories. My part is that of foil or authority figure, the one who was never to find out. They have mapped out the territory without my help, and the density with which their bodies walk these blocks and own this turf accrues from such mapping, not from all my warnings and worryings over the years. There are no clothes chutes to their tale, no stale cigars or miracles performed by Saint Anthony, but the dynamics are the same: bodies enjoined by memories to a place that takes on the feel of family by the fact of its various explorations and tamings. And one day, I know it as a fact and not just an idle fantasy, they will bring their children back to this neighborhood to stare and wonder, point and remember, and then, they won't know why and their children won't know why, I will have moved from the tangent and periphery to the center. It will be because I am absent, I am somewhere else, I am gone or dead, but in their return I will stretch out and hover everywhere, a lost thing found, and their memory of the father will be inextricable from their memory of the place.

Nebraska

I have never been to Nebraska. This is both the challenge and the scandal, then: to describe this place, not as a state or even as a state of mind, but as the place where Alice is, the state that both nurtures and imprisons her, her and her divided double devotion to aging father on a disappearing farm and struggling, not-yet-set daughter in Lincoln. The Cornhusker State gives way to the more figurative totems of duty and devotion, both survived by a monumental sense of humor in a place that is as harsh and unforgiving as it is beautiful. It's not unusual that we think we know a place by knowing a person in that place. What is unusual is that I have only actually seen Alice one more time than I have seen Nebraska, which is to say one single time.

The story bears repeating, and from two different directions. After the collapse of my marriage, I wasn't able to sleep at night. I kept waking up in the middle of the night with solutions to the breakup of the marriage, even though I had tried everything, or other careers I might try. One night I woke in the middle of the night on the verge of tears. Desperately, I needed to think of someone or something that had once made me laugh, that was laughter itself, the memory of laughter. I thought of Alice. That morning, I tracked her down like a long-distance detective: I summoned up my courage and I called her.

Twenty years ago, I gave a paper at a Popular Culture conference in Milwaukee. I was a graduate student then, and it looked good on one's dossier to have attended conferences and to have given papers. I was part of a film panel, and my paper was a definition of cult films (the relationship between outrageous content, innovative style, and the test of time, as I recall).

It was late spring, but the wind was still blowing wintry cold off the lake and over Milwaukee: a wind to keep the city clean, a chill to make the shorewalk deserted. I went to the opening night banquet at the university and looked for other film scholars. I didn't find any. Either they were late coming or were not coming at all. Mix of trip fatigue and the glaze of alienation I always feel the first time I'm in a new and strange city, my mood took me away from the banquet and toward the water. I walked, the water on my right, the skyline on my left, until my cheeks hurt and my nose was running with the cold. We usually think of conferences as the chance to meet new people, but for me part of every going has always been the getting there, marking the territory, being alone long enough to "tame" it, and then the people.

I wasn't a regular attendee at Popular Culture conferences. I didn't even know if I believed in popular culture as a site for academic study. But I was a film teacher/student, films were always a big part of such conferences, and the conferences were always very big anyway, maybe a hundred different panels in those days, so I went. I thought it fitting that such a conference should take place in Milwaukee, site of so many breweries, the hundreds of little bars a necessary outlet for so much beer.

My panel took place on the first day. It went well. I don't remember a single thing about it, so it must have been an average panel: no great papers, no horrible papers. Afterward, several of us, all men, went out to eat a few blocks away from the conference. I remember that the waitresses were topless, and our waitress was especially friendly to us, laughing at our jokes and telling jokes herself. One of the men in our party asked her what she was doing after work. She said she was just about to get off work, and his eyes lit up like fire engines. I found it funny to see a bearded and bespectacled academic face light up with lust like that. She added that she was going off to her second job as a projectionist in one of the movie theaters downtown. Another "match." We were straight from a film panel, she was a film projectionist, but that was about all they had in common. She said she was a big John Travolta fan and did we like him? Well, my colleague, whom I had just met at the panel, was willing to rethink Travolta, even though his paper had been on *Nanook of the North*. So, he left us, going off with the now fully dressed waitress for two showtimes of *Patton* and who knows what afterward. He was a little tipsy when he left, and we all made bets he would fall asleep during the second showing.

The rest of us walked back to the conference hotel and stopped at a nearby bar for a beer. Here there was a stage for go-go dancers, several ladder poles they shimmied up and down (again, the fire engine motif). Where the customers sat was a two-tiered affair: a ground floor, lower than the stage, followed by a raised platform of more tables at eye level with the stage. I nursed my one beer, got bored with the dancers, and couldn't hear my colleagues talk for all the noise. I happened to turn around, and behind us, at the first table of the elevated balcony section, sat one of the most stunningly beautiful women I had ever seen. It was her face that took me over: long, deep black hair that fell lower than her shoulders, active, playful eyes that seemed to be dancing as she talked to her friends, a smile that lit up her whole face and mine as well a table below. She looked exotic. In another city and in another place, other than a bar, she had the skin to be native Hawaiian or Eurasian. Here she looked like an American Indian. I had this sudden surge of warmth and tingling in my stomach, an embarrassed blushing on my face. The French call this *coup de foudre* ("lightning bolt"), their term for love at first sight. I checked my beer. The glass was half-full. It wasn't the beer. I was wearing my glasses, so it wasn't blindness, although I felt blinded. I liked it that she wasn't just sitting still, beautiful statuary, that her face was animated, her gestures animated.

I was nervous, afraid one of my colleagues might be seeing in my face the undoing I had seen in the other man's face. Was I merely feeling the same thing? Lust? I thought not. I just desperately wanted to meet her, have more of a connection than this passing glance, get closer to that smile of hers, close enough that I could put away my glasses (vanity) and still see it. I asked permission of the others to invite her and her party to join us. If any of them had objected, I would have been satisfied. Nobody objected. And since I had made it public, now I had to follow through. It took me another half hour to summon up enough courage to ask our waitress to ask them to join us. To my surprise, they accepted.

Now there were seven of us at two tables pushed together. It was as though she knew the invitation had come from me, intended for her, because she sat down next to me. She was wearing a suit, jacket and pants, with a white blouse, lacy at the collar and down the front for the buttons. The whiteness of her blouse told me the suit wasn't exactly white, although I don't know what color it was. Not white, not exactly cream, not beige, not gray, but a color that could pass for a shade of all of those. And then the western boots. She said her name was Alice.

When you call a person from out of the past, twenty years out of the past, someone you only knew for one night to begin with, you have to expect the entire spectrum of reactions. She doesn't remember you. She remembers you, but too vaguely for there to be a point in calling. She gets angry that you've called, for no other reason than to say you remembered laughing with her. She gets accusatory and wants to know why you're calling now after so many years. She hangs up on you, thinking it's a crank call. She is married. She is a lesbian now. She is dying.

I was prepared for every reaction, but the one I got, which was immediate joy, instant warmth, easy talk and laughter, lots of laughing, as though it had been a matter of days since the last time. I have my speech prepared, but I never get to it. We're already laughing so much it seems redundant to say I've called to remember the laughter.

Her voice is the same as I remembered it: thick and dark and deep, like gourmet chocolate. And since her voice has not changed, I can imagine the rest of her has not changed as well. This is off-logic, I know. It belongs with the same logic that says when you take off your glasses and can't see anybody else, they can't see you either, so you're free to be however you want to be in such relative invisibility, invisibility here roughly translating to anonymity. It is the same off-logic, but it puts me at ease, so I accept it. She still laughs mightily in the middle of sentences, and

I go with her, go with the laughter, do not wait for the punch line, which is worth the wait, warrants her laughter, makes me laugh doubly hard in reaction. It is all Nebraska, of course, that alien planet I never went to, whose reality is stranger to me than Dorothy's Oz.

Every other year or so over those twenty years, I have sent her a Christmas card, and not once have I gotten an answer. But nor were the cards ever returned with the postal mark "address unknown" or "moved" or "no forwarding address." I have thought for twenty years, thought idly, that she has gotten them, not gotten them, both. She thanks me for the Christmas cards and laughs, the laughter so endearing that it more than makes up for any card I might have gotten.

The awkwardness would seem to be time itself, the twenty years of absence on one side of the ledger, the one night we knew each other on the other. I worry that she must think I am obsessive, that one night without sex stretching out so far. I might be one of those fatal attraction types. I should have called her *before* that film came out. But no. She seems to understand why I have called, and time is itself part of the laughter we share. It turns out in those early years after meeting her when I called and a man answered and I hung up, thinking it was a husband, that it was her father. And it turns out in more recent years when she has tried to call me in answer to the Christmas cards and has gotten a woman's voice and hung up, thinking it was a wife, that it was a baby-sitter. A comedy of errors, a tragedy of timing.

We moved from the bar to the hotel room she shared with the other woman at her table. I hadn't even noticed another woman there. They have both come from Lincoln, graduate students at the University of Nebraska. Once we got outside, I noticed the other woman more, because she seemed determined not to let me walk alone with Alice. She left the man who appeared to be her date or her friend, so as to walk with us.

I asked Alice what her paper was about. It was about deer hunting etiquette in Nebraska. At first, I thought she was putting me on. A paper on deer hunting codes at an academic conference in Milwaukee? She was not only serious, she was getting it published. The topic of the paper seemed to fit the boots she was wearing, but not the rest of her. She was elegant and graceful in her body movements, refined in her speech and vocabulary, but underneath all of that, it turned out she was an athletic woman, a longtime tomboy, a rider of horses, a hiker, a roughhouse, frolicsome farm girl of staunch-Catholic Polish parents.

There was this paradox about her: she seemed shy about eye contact and personal space, but she wasn't shy about talking. She seemed to rev up once we got inside the room and she had pulled off her boots. She was ready to tell us Nebraska, stories of the Plains, stories of the farm, her relatives, the animals, especially the intermating of dogs and coyotes, the Pawnee and "crazies," the droughts and crop failures and foibles, all of it black-humorous and absurdly funny. I noticed that she didn't tell much about herself in that telling, no reference to her personal life, her social life, her love life. Instead, "disasters" of Nebraska, one after the other. The other two men from the film panel and I had tears in our eyes from laughing. She was quite willing to stop from time to time, but the spell she had cast was already better than a home fire, a good book, or any other substitute, so we all urged her on. Her friend Marian just raised her eyebrows from time to time, as though she already knew all the stories, was mildly distanced or disapproving of this telling of them, or maybe she was just tired, wanted all of us to leave so she could go to sleep.

I had a knot in my stomach from so much laughing. I had to go to the bathroom often, each trip prolonged longer than I should have waited, because I didn't want to miss anything. Alice erupted in her own laughter, often after the verbs and before the ends of sentences. We waited while she laughed, laughed with her, got the point she was laughing at, and laughed again. Her laugh wasn't a giggle exactly, not a twitter either, but rather an uproarious ripple of laughter, smooth as water running over rocks, full of her throat, breasts, and stomach, the whole upper half of her going into her laughter.

The stories themselves were weird and quirky, often with a peppering of cruelty to them: an uncle losing his leg in the thrashing machine; a horse, blind in one eye, always running into the barn from the blind side, good only for going to the right; the old schoolhouse with the rule of one-family recesses, because more than that would mean fights or family feuds. Between the portraits and the punch lines, Alice talked Nebraska. The many concrete details about hiking along the Platte River, about the community of women in a kitchen, cooking roast duck and rabbits for a Polish Thanksgiving, about the stables where the horses were, about her parents planting linden trees for luck, all the descriptive detail or backdrop or setup, these were poetry to me, because they were all foreign. I had no hands-on experience with any of them. She described them casually, even hastily, as though she were in a hurry to get to the funny parts, but she described them vividly enough for me to transport myself, to inhabit what I had never seen. I thought of detective novels in which I could forgive a patness of plot, trick turns, and a collapse of credibility if the procedural

aspects were there: the routines of stakeouts, the internal work-
ings of a system, the step-by-step projections of a detective's mind
thinking *like* the serial killer, needing finally to risk it all, take the
plunge, "become" the killer to catch the killer. The narrative drive
in such descriptions, the feel of scaffolding becoming inhabitable
buildings, the birth of things before they got moved around as plot
pieces, these things Alice did well. They made her stories longer,
of course, but they also infused the tales with a folkloric voyeur-
ism, a fall-back depth, so that the funny parts were not sniper's
potshots but rather richly layered, textured, *mano a mano*, and yet
tender, quarter always given, whether asked for or not. She spoke
about these people naturalistically, Zola with a sense of humor, as
though Nebraska had formed them during the Stone Age and the
process of fossilization were still going on in the one-crop farms
of today. She spoke about them as an insider who had gotten out
and was now going back in again for the retelling.

We finish the phone call awkwardly, the
only moment of awkwardness, not because there is anything
wrong, but because we don't know how to wind it up after twenty
years. We don't know how to say goodbye. I think afterward that
the lack of closure is what has kept her alive in my memory all
these years. Narrative drive, because it is a drive, stops awkwardly
and incompletely.

I think of a film I teach often, Chris Marker's *La Jetée*, in which
a man with a strong mental image of his past time-travels to be
with a woman. Phrases come to me. "From a truth too fantastic
to be believed . . ." Gradually, the shock (impossibility) of time
travel dissipates, gives way to a building, a slow construction of

their time together. I think of Alice this way. The shock of this call has already passed.

Slowly, over several calls, I try to move the narratives. She is still adept, quite skilled at telling Nebraska, but I want more of her, her personal life, the missing and unspoken spots, the deep dark secrets. She is still shy about herself, or maybe indirection is the Nebraska way, I don't know which. What I find out, I find out in spurts, little by little, and only in response to direct questions.

There are no dark secrets, just the constant onslaught of blizzards in the winter months, the aging of everyone around her, the care she needs to give them. She had been married and divorced at the time I met her. Abandoned by her husband, she went back to school, leaving her infant daughter with her parents.

The daughter is now almost grown, a student at the University of Nebraska in Lincoln. Alice continues to teach at a branch campus, giving most of what she makes to her daughter for tuition and living expenses. Alice's mother is dead now. Her father is alive, in his eighties, still on the family farm. When I ask Alice about friends, she mentions a couple, then she says two good friends have moved away, two others have died. Marian is one of the two who died.

"She was a good friend," Alice says. "She was very protective of me."

Finally, Marian had had enough and she ordered all of us out. I didn't want the night to end, but I didn't quite know how to engineer its continuation. Others left the room first, and just as I was about to ask Alice if she wanted to go out for coffee, she asked me instead. I was grateful that it happened that way, gracefully, with no awkwardness beyond Marian's raised eyebrows that Alice was going out again.

It was four in the morning, and few places were open. Finally, we found an all-night diner where she got a carton of milk and I got an iced tea to go. We walked slowly. There were some silences, but I didn't find them uncomfortable. When I talked, I realized that she was hearing me for the first time.

She tells me Nebraska leads the nation in attempts to censor books, and she is a lover of books. She belongs to four different book clubs. She says this is what educated women do in Nebraska. She tells me she met Jerzy Kosinski, who came to Nebraska to fight the attempted censorship of his novel *Being There*. She got herself a press pass and met him and his wife. She says he told her he might come back someday to write about the Poles on the Plains. We laugh.

She tells me her brother is coming to the farm that weekend with his friend, the former U-2 pilot, who is still getting lost. They have to allow extra time when they hunt: the time to hunt and the time to find the friend.

She tells me she has gone to a college "fair," representing her university at a stall, one booth among the many, at which prospective students can come ask questions, interview, take away application forms. Next to Alice is a man representing the college program in Swine Management. He wonders why he isn't more successful at recruiting. She tells him a yearly salary of ten thousand dollars for an eight- to ten-hour day at a slaughterhouse might not seem that attractive to a high school student. He wears a button on his lapel with a smiling pig on it.

These are the ongoing Disasters of Nebraska stories. But interspersed with them, now that she knows me a little bit, are the stories of hard times. The farm has fallen on hard times. Her father has lost one of their farms and has had to mortgage another. There are no more horses. Alice talks about how she used to love to ride them, then says she doesn't think she'll ever be able to ride again. The gifts from her youth are now almost all gone.

The price for keeping her father's dignity, for keeping him on his farm, is Alice. She goes to him every weekend, bringing the week's food, cooking and cleaning for him. She leaves him her VCR, so he can have movies, but this means she has no VCR for herself at her apartment. She drives a twelve-year-old car, which stalls frequently, dies every blizzard, but she can't afford to get another. She gives most of her money to her daughter in college. She gives most of her time and body to her aging father.

"How did I get myself into this?" she asks, not especially of me, for it is clear to me she's been asking the question so long that it sounds like "How do I get myself out of this?"

She speaks of personal deprivation almost to the point of whining, then apologizes for complaining so much, asks me if it annoys me. It doesn't. I am single-parenting three sons. I understand duty. There are plug-in cliches for this. I think of one from my grandmother: we have to play the cards we're dealt. Life is essentially unfair, sometimes radically unfair, not even close to balancing out.

We have both become college teachers, but here again life isn't fair. I teach two courses a semester; she teaches five. I am rewarded for all my publications; she doesn't have time to write. I have an office with a computer, all the amenities. She doesn't even have an office. She sits at her desk, wide open to students or colleagues, no privacy, constant interruptions. I teach summer school every summer for extra money. She teaches summer school every summer because it is required, part of her yearly salary.

I keep thinking: why would anyone ever go to Nebraska, let alone live there an entire lifetime? On one phone call, she answers me. She has had the flu, a flat tire, three winter storms in one week, countless committees and nonstop nighttime grading of student compositions, she has complained about all of this in great detail, and then she stops herself.

"You know," she says, "Nebraska is the most beautiful place on earth in spring and summer."

It's the other side of the Disasters Stories, the side I never hear, and I encourage her to tell me more. She tells me about some of the rivers near the farm, about Indian burial grounds, the Black Hills of the Dakotas, all God's earth in one place, made so desperately uninhabitable by the winter storms, bad economy, lack of jobs, and poverty-scale wages, all of them as though required to keep the squatters from everywhere else away.

"I'm stuck," she says and laughs. Stuck in that place. Stuck on that place.

Time moves on: a cliché whose cruelty is ever fresh. Time, the vehicle of memory, plaything of memory, is also the enemy of memory. After ten or twelve calls in all, Alice and I are caught up on our news and complete with each other. In time the one night long ago will merge with the calls of twenty years later. I think now that Alice represents the memory of uncontrollable laughter, a memory of the body heaving, laughing spasmodically, aided no doubt by the fact I knew nothing about the people or places of Nebraska, laughter as a superiority reflex and compensation for ignorance. Laughter, like grief, cannot be described from inside, when one is in the throes of it, but I do believe it can be remembered, bodily so, even when the particulars of what was laughed at have long been forgotten. The proof: we are predisposed to laugh when we are around people we know have made us laugh in the past. Contact high. Instant laughter. And when the memory itself has faded, there is still the laughter of the memory, just as in winter, underneath the surface ice, there is still the lake. Laughter, then, is memory without content, a koan, the sound of one hand clapping, an antidote to aging.

The Roy Stories

We call them the "Roy stories," my sons and I. We've always called them that. The ritual for bedtime stories in the dark has been that my sons request either a story about when they were babies or a story about when I was a boy with my friend Roy at the cottage on the lake in Michigan. When they were very little, they wanted only the Roy stories. Now that they're teenagers and have some distance from their own childhoods, and the prerequisite loss of memory that comes with that distance, they are more interested in their own "baby" stories than they are in me and Roy. But for years it was Roy and me they wanted, and the stories always began this way: "Roy and me were walking down the cottage road . . ."

I never had a story ready. I knew what was coming, their request for one, but I never prepared the stories in advance. Maybe this was my own challenge, to keep me interested in telling them. And so suddenly each night I had to remember one or make one up on the spot, and the trick in the telling was to disguise the made-up ones, to make my sons believe they were the real ones.

"Let's see now. Roy and me were walking down the cottage road . . ."

There were very few rules to these stories, other than that they had to be funny in some way and I had to outsmart Roy by story's end. Roy, as I remembered him and as I described him to my sons, was not so different from Sluggo in the *Nancy* comics. He was short, a year younger than I was, had little hair (what we used to call a short butch haircut, what my sons now call a butthead cut), had freckles and buck teeth, wore dirty T-shirts, bragged a lot, and always got us in some kind of trouble.

We did what boys of ten and eleven usually do on a lake: we fished and swam, we spied on girls, we went exploring in the woods, we played baseball in the backyard, we heckled farmers in their pickup trucks, we chased after some kids and got chased a lot by other kids, depending on the age and size of the other kids. We looked for ways to make money (selling lemonade or miniature furniture we had made by the side of the road), ways to "explore" (building tree huts or rafts), ways to grow up faster (pestering older teenage girls at other cottages), and ways to test our parents (getting "lost," not coming back from walks to the dam in time for meals, sneaking bread to feed the fish, buying too much candy in town). By today's standards we were relatively harmless in our pranks and exploits. We could be gone for hours at a time, get into a little trouble without it escalating into a lot of trouble, not be with gangs, not do drugs, not shoplift, and so forth. But for my small sons in the city, we were the equivalent of Tom Sawyer and Huck Finn, leading lives full of daily mysteries.

For a brief spell, I thought I should have a "moral" to my tales, some kind of lesson in growing up for my boys to fall asleep with, some kind of caveat: see, we did this, and look what trouble we got into, so you better never do this yourselves. But I had no flair for being Aesop. My boys quickly saw through these exemplary fictions and demanded another Roy story that was funnier, no should or shouldn't attached.

During another phase I took my cue from the books we read that lead up to the bedtime stories in the dark. If Babar fell and bruised his knee, I made up a story about Roy falling too. If Pinocchio's father got swallowed by a whale, I made up a story about catching a large-mouthed bass that had swallowed a tennis shoe. If the North-going Zax and South-going Zax wouldn't budge in Dr. Seuss, I made up a story about a right-of-way dispute between some older boys named Perry and Hostile and Roy and me (Roy having caused the trouble in the first place by mouthing off to the older boys). In that particular story, we got away by telling the older boys to look up at the plane in the sky (which wasn't there), then diving between their legs and "winning" the dispute that way. In story terms we had won and they had to acknowledge our cleverness. In real life, if Roy and I had gone between the legs of any older boys, they would have chased us until they caught us or darkness, whichever came first. But the muddiness of meaning in real life, the lingering conflicts that don't get resolved, the long periods of boredom between adventures, these were all edited out of the stories, and my sons silently concurred in the editing. Once they caught on that I was taking my cues from the books, they stopped me and told me to start over with a new story that had nothing to do with Babar, Pinocchio, or Dr. Seuss. On the other hand, if I told them a slice-of-life story, without the humor of a punch line or other dramatic ending, they ridiculed my story, said it didn't count, and demanded another.

"One day Roy and me were walking down the cottage road . . ."

There are only so many "fantastic" animals one can meet on a cottage road, only so many detours one can take, only so many fish one can catch. Gradually, I had to invent new characters to keep the plots going. The real Roy and I wished to desperation that we had girlfriends. In the stories we had them. Mine was Becky:

stolen, no doubt, from Tom Sawyer, and she was smart, pretty, and good at sports. Roy's girlfriend was Doreen, who was taller than any of the rest of us, loyal to Becky, surly and cantankerous, as likely to give Roy a swift kick in the derriere as a hug or a hand to hold. My boys didn't want "romance" in those early years anyway; they much preferred the battle of the sexes, and they laughed every time Roy took a beating at the hands of Doreen as long as Becky remained nice to me.

Then more characters evolved. The favorite for my boys was a tomboy named Agnes, who came to be known in the stories as Baggy Aggie, because she always wore her older sister's sweatshirts. Aggie could outfish us any day of the week, had even less patience for Roy than Doreen did, and was always trying to come between me and Roy, not because she wanted to be my girlfriend, but because she wanted to be my buddy in baseball, fishing, and swimming. So Roy and Aggie told elaborate lies about each other, lies to make my boys laugh: Roy said Aggie put spider webs in her hair; Aggie said Roy ate worms; Roy said Aggie never used a Kleenex when she sneezed; Aggie said Roy never wiped himself after going to the bathroom. It didn't matter what the lie was, the more elaborate the better. My boys were glad for any stories that contained Baggy Aggie.

I was careful all along not to include too many stories that contained my brothers and sisters, because I knew my boys would ask them to verify the stories sooner or later. My brothers and sisters remembered Roy, his buck teeth, his snotty disposition, his bragging, and that was enough to keep my boys satisfied and keep the saga going for years.

On our summer visits to the same lake, the boys asked me to point out certain cottages, places in the woods, icons from the stories. More, they wanted to emulate feats from the stories. If

Roy and I were able to swim across the lake, they wanted to do the same thing, and at a much younger age. If Roy and I had caught twenty perch one night by using red licorice twizzlers for bait, they wanted to stay out in the boat until they had topped our catch. If Roy and I had been allowed to go to evening dances in the garage by the dam, they wanted to go out at night and scare up their own dance at the dam. The degree to which they wanted to emulate the stories or better them was testimony to the power of the stories in the first place.

"One day Roy and me were walking down the cottage road . . ."

My boys insisted that we walk as a family down the cottage road, looking for misadventures. When nobody special happened to cross our path, they made up people. Their mischief consisted of putting rocks in people's mailboxes, lighting sparklers, catching fireflies, and chasing occasional rabbits. I think they were disappointed that "now" time was not nearly as exciting as olden days and that something essential, something powerful, had died between the time of my childhood and theirs. Still, they held on to the hope that a deer might suddenly dart across our path, a rattlesnake might wander out of the woods after a rainstorm, or that we might even meet a grown-up Baggy Aggie or Roy. After all, if we could return every summer to the lake, why couldn't they?

I knew why. There weren't any jobs to be had in that part of Michigan, so devoid of any industry except the tourist industry. Young people here grew up and went out of state to college, if they could, or joined the army. The exodus out left the lake somehow smaller, shallower, weedier. Cottages that were once getaways for whole families from Saginaw, Midland, Detroit, and Lansing on weekends now bore the scars of time: no more children, a widow or widower, year-round living, people like my father who went out to grocery-shop, play golf, or go to church but who had stopped using the lake long ago.

There are many stories about me and Roy that I haven't told my boys, either because Roy cursed too much in them or because the fistfights ended badly or because the misadventures with girls seemed "too old" for my sons. Roy *was* my best summer friend, but during the school year we never wrote or called each other. He was a best friend "of place," which is to say, by default. In those tall tales I told my boys, we were always closer, like blood brothers, idealized best friends.

The truth about Roy doesn't fit the telling of tales. He was often spiteful and mean-spirited. I now suspect he was abused or at least occasionally beaten by his parents, because he was often cruel to animals, and I had to talk him out of pouring glue in the mouths of cats and putting cherry bombs in a bird's nest. He could turn on people the way German shepherds sometimes turn on their masters: suddenly and without apparent provocation. His sexual fantasies ran more toward window peeping after someone had taken a swim than the innocent hand holding at the dam. In our teenage years, we grew apart little by little, as I had different girlfriends each summer and he withdrew. He ran away from home a couple of times. Then abruptly, one summer when we arrived in June, he wasn't there. His family had sold the cottage. There was a new family there, one with three daughters. I should have minded more than I did. He and I had spent a lot of time together. But two of those three daughters were near my age and very pretty, so I welcomed the change. I asked them what happened to the family that sold them the cottage. One answer I got was that Roy's father had gotten a job in Lansing. Another answer was that the father went to a job in Lansing, while Roy and his mother went somewhere else. Many years later, I saw one of the girls we used to pester in the grocery store in town, and I asked her if she knew what had happened to Roy, since my boys were always asking. She said she thought he had gone to Vietnam. She wasn't sure he had ever come back. She was appalled that I would tell young children stories about "that creep." There's a tragedy in the truth somewhere, but I don't know the details and can't seem to find them out.

One of my first cottage girlfriends, when I was leaving Roy for girlfriends, came by our cottage last summer with two of her sons. She was asking for donations to help get some of the stumps removed from the lake. I didn't recognize her at first. She had been as skinny as a pencil as a teenager, with black hair done in a pixie, and, it seemed to me then, she had the patent on how to wear tank tops. Now she was slightly obese, with henna hair and a sweatshirt like Baggy Aggie was supposed to have worn. I recognized her through her sons, who were teenage sons and looked like she used to look, only in boys' bodies. She was flattered that I recognized her, and there was an awkward moment or two (she had been one of my first kissing teachers behind the garage down at the dam). We did chitchat reminiscing, gingerly so, telling each other in five minutes what it had taken us both twenty-five years to learn and forget, and I asked her if she knew what had happened to Roy. She didn't remember him at first.

"Didn't he have something wrong with him that stunted his growth?" she asked.

No, I didn't believe so.

Well, she didn't remember the name, but she remembered the buck teeth and how obnoxious he was. She remembered that she would have seen more of me if she hadn't seen me so often with him, and she thought for the longest time that I must be cocky and obnoxious too. Then she said her friend Doreen hated him even more than she had. I don't ever remember her having a friend named Doreen, but I had to smile anyway, because tall tales have a way of going round and round until they one day become truth claims.

"One day me and Roy were walking down the cottage road . . ." It's not *Don Quixote*, not even *Catcher in the Rye*, but it is our family bedtime saga, and it derives from the same pool of the picaresque: adventures as big as our imaginations, imaginations bigger than our appetites, appetites bigger than our common sense. Sprinklings of cursings, boastings, pratfalls, and moral lessons. The Roy stories have them all.

I don't mind at all when nothing eventful happens on my walks with my sons down the cottage road. It's enough to look deep into those pine trees, listen to the whistling poplars in the wind, hear dogs barking over the next hill, and feel the chilly dirt of the cottage road on my bare feet. From the parent's point of view, nothing happening is the best story of all.

And my sons, now that they are teens, don't look for similarities any longer between my childhood cottage road and theirs. They don't want to know that Roy was cruel to animals or that he might have died in Vietnam. They keep him as grown-up children keep Santa Claus, the Easter Bunny, the tooth fairy—as diminished fact of life overlaying unlimited fantasy. The distance between those two isn't simply one traversed by memory, good memory or bad, but something like the first taste of death and dying, the hors d'oeuvres of mortality. Perhaps that is why they have shifted their interest from the Roy stories to stories of their own childhood, and even when I have run out of true stories about them and make them up, they still don't know the difference, or if they do, they're too sleepy to let on. One day soon they will stop asking for stories altogether. They will have enough sophisticated doses of Shakespeare in the schools and Stephen King at home that they will become jaded, cynical, disbelieving simpler home-spun tales, even when they are the heroes and main characters. They will then go through a drought, a period of hibernation, filled with best-sellers, great books and movies, distant tales by other tellers, and then one day they will have their own children. The cycle will begin again: the children's books of that time versus the stories they will remember or make up; the stories of their childhood versus the stories of their children's childhoods. I like to think this cycle of fact giving way to falsehood, rising interest and slack, belief and disbelief, and finally the relationship of stories to impending sleep and dreams, is the cycle of life itself.

Maine

I've been to Maine for a month: not long, not nearly long enough, but long enough for it to make sense to me that a Texan president should call Maine his home. Bangor to Bar Harbor, Presque Isle to Portland, the cities are small, tucked in, away from the world, rolled up like the sleeves of a giant lumberjack. The influence of French Canada sags like an inverted umbrella over Maine: the bilingual signs, the backwoods feel of junk stores (called "antiques") snuggled in a cutaway patch of pine trees, a hunter's English spoken haltingly by bearded men in plaid jackets. Maine is dirt-poor and stately both, the poverty in the people, the elegance in the landscape. Time is always time gone by, the mood away from Massachusetts that of solitude, anonymity, interiority. Maine is a move-to place, a getaway hide-out/refuge/haven for other New Englanders, a lazy, idle-down listening place, a nesting place for old hippies, artists, spartans, and loons.

I remember best the loons. These are creatures with Canadian passports, who sneak across the border in pairs, pick a lake, and fight for their lives to keep the lake. They are territorial to the extreme, arch and antisocial in their behavior to all but their mates and offspring. Within their "nuclear" family, they are gentle, playful, patient. They mate for life. They piggyback their young until their young are big enough to swim for themselves. They make themselves scarce during the day, hiding or sleeping, away from the boaters and hunters. At night they come out to frolic. They look gangly, goofy, and awkward: hence the phrase "crazy as a loon." But they are anything but. They emit their intricate loon song all night long, using the reverberations as "radar" to move through the water, which movement is otherwise silent, effortless, leaving no ripple or wake.

I lay in my bed on the banks of Lake Wesserrunsett outside Skowhegan and listened to the loons for hours. I was amazed at the loon song, raucous and melodic at the same time, mix of aria and ambulance siren, each loon assigned a frequency, a range of notes not to be duplicated by any other loon, the utterance and its immediate answer both ersatz and in harmony. The notes seemed to move, rootless by the time they reached me. I heard a certain note to the left of my bed, then to the right, then close to the bank, then far off. I could not imagine the logic or pattern, and I began to suspect the loons of ventriloquism, as though, even under the protective blanket of darkness, they had to throw their voices for safety's sake.

Some people want to shoot the loons, in anger for the loss of sleep. I had no such anger. I grew up listening to owls hoot, frogs croak, cicadas cackle like castanets. Listening to loons was simply another form of night music, and once I had grown accustomed to them, they seemed as lyrical and lonesome, as magical and melancholy, as night freight trains in the Midwest, passing with a whistle instead of a stop. Instead of *trying* to sleep, I got up, half-naked, and with my blanket as a shawl, I went to the rocking chair on the porch and listened, as though to a soothing baseball game on the radio, as though to a good book, without the eye strain.

We bring to a new place all those comparisons with our past, with which to familiarize the new place, to tame it, and so I brought my memories of Michigan with a time warp. It seemed to me that Maine was now what Michigan used to be when I was a child: the same clean lakes, the same scrubby pines, the same mix of French names and Indian names, the same overflow of Canadian influence and outdoors orientation. Instead of Skowhegan: Muskegon, Tawas, Interlochen. Instead of Presque Ile: Au Gres, Charlevoix, Sault Ste. Marie. All of the comparisons held true, except for the loons. I remember Canada geese, even some errant ducks, but I never saw a single loon on the lake in Michigan.

I went from Maine to Michigan, and it seemed to me that the comparison went from poetic to crude. If Maine was still unexplored and underdeveloped, then Michigan was explored and then forgotten again, gutted somehow of its former innocence. There were plant closings weekly, mismanagement of federal funds, scandals of toxic waste dumpings that kept many of the bays and lakes off-limits. The same roadside commerce of yard sales still took place, but now the boat, the cars, and the house behind the sellers were also for sale. From farms to factories, snowmobiles to cabin cruisers, the whole state was for sale. I felt sad at seeing so many "bargains," because it seemed like the heart of a people was for sale.

In that sadness I felt, I put loons on the lakes in Michigan. I had listened closely enough that I had memorized their songs. I sat at the picnic table that hasn't been used for years, its legs a mass of splinters and rotting wood, spider webs in the angles of all the joints, and I looked at my lake with superimposed loons, where there used to be speedboats and teenagers proving their mettle on water skis, rafts to swim to, nightly dances at the dam. The lake now reeked of peace and quiet, neglect, and too many retirees who never left their cottages. I had known the children of these people, dated them and danced with them, and a FOR SALE sign here meant that the parents had moved away or the parent had died, and their grown-up children weren't coming back.

The evening breezes lack the force of breezes off the Atlantic, the storms are more surly here, tornado induced, and the race of people seems more fragile in Michigan, but the loons take to the superimposition anyway. Maybe they complain of the tameness in their songs, but they have fewer territorial fights and an easier time of swimming and finding food than they had in Maine. They piggyback their young in relative privacy, and the shoreline is less rocky, so maybe they air-dry themselves in the sand while we're sleeping. Maybe they even wander up as far as the picnic table, throwing their voices back to the lake, so I'll think they're still in the water.

The loons from Maine have allowed me to forgive Michigan its fall from grace, the hard edges it has gotten since my childhood. Maybe, it occurs to me, this is the best form of travel, when we take back with us something as intangible as loon music and use it to retame and reanimate the places we come from.

Homesickness

It is the year of the ram for some, the year of the Persian Gulf War for most, but this has been the year of Mexico for me and my sons. Ian, my ninth grader, went on a month-long exchange to Tlaxcala. David, my seventh grader, went on a five-day holiday to Cancun. Daniel, my fifth grader, went on a three-week exchange to Cuernavaca. They are all safely back, full of ponchos and serapes, stories of visiting archaeological ruins and bartering at the local *mercados*, and we are now preparing ourselves for the return exchanges of their Mexican host "brothers."

While they were gone, I became more pensive, more withdrawn. I thought it would have been the other way around. I had sudden free time to go to movies and restaurants, time to seek out friends and do things, but I didn't. I stayed home and thought a lot. The ceilings seemed higher, the walls seemed wider, the whole apartment stretched out in their absence, and I walked the hallway without resistance or encounters. I thought to myself: this is the beginning of the "empty nest." I thought: I will look back on this time as the time when they began to leave me. At the same time, my missing them was cushioned quite a bit by the realization of what incredible experiences they were having, what a good thing it was that their schools offered and sanctioned such exchanges for people this young. I supported their going wholeheartedly and kept my moments of heavy heart to myself.

I supported them, because I too had gone on foreign exchange programs as a student. For me these programs came much later. In retrospect, my whole student career was geared around them. I chose the University of Michigan as my college because it offered a junior year abroad program in France. I knew I would go on that program while I was still a junior in high school. All I wanted to do in school was learn languages and travel: speak foreign languages, be somewhere else, be *someone* else. I majored in languages and took overloads to fit in my French, Spanish, and Russian. I lived in the dorms to save money, did not pledge a fraternity because I would be gone, worked as a short-order cook and photographer at proms, frat parties, and weddings, all to have money in Europe. When I came back from my year in France, I turned around and went to Spain on a Fulbright year. I came back from that year proficient in travel and languages, and almost by default I went to graduate school in comparative literature, because it was a program in which I could use my various languages. I didn't go to school, then, very sanely, in the sense that I never carved out for myself a career calculated to get me a good job at high pay. I used school to go abroad and learn languages.

When I left for France, I was the first of the seven children in my family to go off anywhere far or for very long. With six other children still at home, my parents were hardly devastated with the prospects of the empty nest. But it was the beginning of the empty nest for me, from the child's point of view. I looked upon my year abroad as the rite of passage between boyhood and manhood, as the final "break" from parents and siblings, as a kind of "statement" that I was different from them. I went "native" in France, giving myself over to a life of fervent interest in politics, afternoon talks at outdoor cafés and bistros, dressed in turtleneck pullovers and gray flannel pants, a book of Sartre or Malraux in hand, a season's pass to the *cinémathèque* and all the latest films by Resnais and Godard. I had wine on my breath and francs in my pocket, I lived within walking distance of Mont Sainte-Victoire, the mountain made famous by Cezanne, I laughed at the nasal twang of the Midi merchants, unbuttoned my shirt to the evening gale of Mistral winds, and thought I was a citizen of the world.

I refused to speak English with anyone. One day on the Cours Mirabeau some Mormon boys on mission there passed me with a sign that read: IF YOU CAN READ THIS, SMILE! I couldn't help myself. I smiled, not because the sign told me to, but because the sign was so ludicrous and unexpected. They followed me. I pretended not to know any English, but they had seen me smile. They persisted. Finally, I gave in. They became my friends that year, but they were the only exceptions, people with whom I would speak in my native tongue.

I remember having incredible bouts of loneliness that came and went like flu. My French friends would say: "Ah, tu as le cafard." They told me I was homesick before I would think it myself. What did it mean to be homesick? Did it mean I missed my parents, my brothers and sisters, my college friends? Did it mean I missed winter snow, football games, hamburgers and milkshakes? I could have called home but didn't. I could have sought out other Americans but didn't. La Rotonde on the Cours Mirabeau served American-style hamburgers and french fries, and they even had

American catsup. I went there, but I only filled my stomach, not my heart. What did it mean to be homesick, then?

I wrote letters home, dutifully, once a week, letters that were more descriptive than emotional. I recounted my weekend trip to the Alps in a Deux Chevaux, hitchhiking to Arles, the bridge at Avignon. I told them about playing cards with Corsicans, dipping my feet in the fountains, meeting Arab street sweepers at night. But I never just told them how I was feeling. My mother wrote back, dutifully, once a week, and her letters were about winter blizzards, canning jam, the car not starting, my brothers playing basketball, my sister's toothache. I remember her using the same formulaic lines over and over: "There's not much to tell really, just wanted to get this off to you." At holiday times, especially Christmas, and around birthdays, yes, then I really missed home in a bodily way, and I think they must have missed me most at those times too. My father's one warning was not to come home married. My mother's one warning was not to come home with malnutrition.

Over the years I've come to think that homesickness is a form of grief that has no real object. It's a mind-set that has no materialistic cure. I was so sad to leave France that it got in the way of my being glad to be back home. My family welcomed me back in their way, which meant that they weren't especially curious to hear about the French, to know any more about my travels, to find out what I was thinking or who I had become. They were more interested in "swallowing" the time gone, in feeding me and seeing me wear blue jeans again, in treating me as though I had never gone away. "Now that you've gotten *that* out of your system," they seemed to be saying, "let's get on with life here." They wanted to know what next, and I honestly didn't know what next. My head was in the past year, not in the year to come. Two or three days after my return, I began to feel that I had never gone, that everything was the same as before, that my mind and body were idling, sputtering, stalling out, and falling back into old habits and ways of being that had nothing to do with my time abroad. And then, strangely, I felt incredibly homesick for France and anything French: the smell of a Gitane cigarette, the sound of Piaf singing, a Cezanne painting, things hard to come by in the middle of Michigan.

I don't think I ever told my parents how much I loved them during that year abroad, and I wonder now if they were waiting, holding out, hoping to hear that. It wasn't that I wanted to deny them such an affirmation of feeling; it was rather that I considered it a given, something already understood between us, and so there was no need to state it. In the years that followed, they never once alluded to the year I was away as "the year I was away" but rather as the ongoing memory of those there, the continuity of memory, uninterrupted by my trip. "You remember such and such," my mother would scold and then stop herself, "oh no, maybe you were gone then." But it was always my catching up to them and their memories, not the other way around.

Twenty-five years later, my sons have gone to Mexico, and I am reminded that I never brought back French gifts for my parents when my sons bring gifts back for me. Daniel gives me dolls and a blanket with lions and tigers on it. David gives me coins, a pewter drinking mug, a slingshot. Ian gives me a throw rug, a doll, a leather billfold, and a slingshot. They've been back for three weeks now and we still haven't sorted out all the stories. One ate fried cactus, stuffed with tomatoes, breadcrumbs, and jalapeños. Another ate chicken with the head still on. One went to Acapulco for the weekend, another to a ranch to ride horses. They talk of making girlfriends, of how sweet the bottled Coca Colas were, of sewer smells, native *dulces* (candies and desserts), falling asleep on Mexican bus rides, getting bit by bugs at night. Ian speaks of teaching English at the *tecnica*, David speaks of drinking sangria at a thatched palapas bar, Daniel talks about his trip to the grottoes and caves at Las Grutas. They all talk about the elaborate masks and costumes they saw for Mardi Gras. They prove to each other that they've learned how to swear in Spanish. They have missed eating hoagies and listening to rap music and playing Sega and Nintendo with their friends, but not at the expense of losing Mexico so quickly. They want me to make sangria. They want their bedtime stories in Spanish. They want to see the Diego Rivera murals at the Art Museum.

For me, the real gifts are not in the things they have brought back but in the things they say and do: not all at once, but one by one, over time and out of earshot of the others. Daniel comes for hugs. "Un fuerte abrazo," he says, and he bearhugs me. During one of these bearhugs, he kisses me on the cheek and whispers in my ear: "This is a Kodak moment." David comes to hold my hand. He says my hands are always warm, as warm as the Cancun sand was on his feet. My hands, his feet, he has found a point of re-entry. And Ian confesses to me that he did feel homesick from time to time. It was always at night when he was in that strange bed, fighting off mosquitoes and finding it difficult to get to sleep. It was then he thought about home. "You know what I did?" he says. "I sang all the songs you used to sing to us when we were kids." The songs he referred to were the songs passed down to me from my mother, her singing and piano playing, my piano playing and then my singing to three small sons in the red rocking chair, them in diapers and on my lap: "Always," "Lavender Blue," "Danny Boy." I wondered what his Mexican family thought, hearing him sing these songs to himself in the dark. I was touched.

In time I will forget which boy gave me which doll or blanket from the trips to Mexico. But I won't soon forget the whisper of a Kodak moment in my ear, hand holding like the sands of Cancun, or the story about the songs I used to sing. They're all examples, no one of them more precious than the other, of something more general that I can't vocalize, something akin to a definition of homesickness, and not just the feeling, but the way through the feeling. We carry the bodies of our loved ones when we go away. We can't produce them on demand like passports, but we carry them as part of our "luggage" just the same. Those bodies seem to disappear and merge with ours; the longer we're away, the more they fade, until finally we seem to lose our grip, and then we hold them as a thought. And maybe homesickness is the fear that we've lost proof, and somehow in our going all that's left over there is our thought, the disembodied thought. The hug, the held hands, and the songs are proofs of substance, ways of putting that fear to rest, putting the thought back into bodies. For these and for all the other nonmaterial gifts my sons give me without giving them a second thought, I am grateful.

The Disappearance of Setting

Politics and setting both are endangered species in fiction. Or when they appear, they're totemic, like the background Commanche and buffalo in westerns, themselves disappearing, all the more precious because they're always on the verge of extinction. My students situate their stories on page one; then, more often than not, the plots are invaded by dialogue like a virus, no known cure. For all they care, I tell them, their stories could have taken place in the K Mart parking lot. I remind them of Joyce's Dublin, Lowry's Mexico, Faulkner's South, Michael Herr's Vietnam. I am still thrilled and thoroughly convinced by the way writers like John McPhee and Barry Lopez make me reside in the places they describe, reside while reading, so that the places—and the politics of place—become dense with temporality, part of point of view, interesting as people.

My students sometimes write about the casually returned Vietnam veteran in their stories. He is generally hip and wasted, living off a woman he doesn't love, doing drugs or remembering doing drugs or trying to avoid doing drugs, still into death and lethal weapons, and fending off flashbacks faster than Faulkner's Quentin. I allow for the age difference between me and my students, and still I scream at them: there is no such animal as a casually returned Vietnam veteran. What distinguishes your vet, I ask, from a beatnik of the fifties, a radical hippie of the sixties, a punk rocker of the seventies? And why do you put him in a fast-sketch jungle that quickly becomes as anonymous as the K Mart parking lot?

I recoil from these stick-figure vets with their wasted faces and worried narcissism. They never live in the present, yet they have come back from the war with no sense of history, no coherent politics, no fight or life force. They occasion flashbacks in which they themselves drop away like so much dry kindling, and the authors intrude, bald-faced, speaking for a posttraumatic stress syndrome they have never experienced. I find such characters pornographic, especially in the way they are myopic about a past that never made sense. The way they cling to buddies and can't have lovers, wives, or children, except in small doses. The way they are plague carriers, doomed to infect everyone around them. They are sick with Vietnam itself, as though it were a disease devoid of any consciousness. The K Mart view of Southeast Asia.

I have always been returning from Vietnam. It is the one experience that most separates me from my father, my brothers and sisters, who stayed home, went to school, or held on to jobs, raised families, and watched the war on television. Vietnam was an interruption in my life of such overriding deferral that my past and future could never be sewn together again. I spent so much time fighting against going that it took more than coming back to come back. Almost twenty years later, it still feels like I am returning from Vietnam.

The fight against going was protracted and complicated. I spent almost six years fighting the draft and trying to stay in graduate school. One year I was first on the waiting list for the reserves at

Fort Benjamin Harrison in Indianapolis, and I wondered why I never got the call. It was discovered that the recruiter was selling places in the reserves, so he and the waiting list were both "discontinued." I went to the air force and applied for its officer training candidate schooling in languages, since I spoke French, Spanish, Russian. The recruiter was delighted, told me I would be going to Texas, and I was to wait for final orders. I was informed by mail that there were no openings at the center in Texas, that the recruiter had misinformed me, and that he had been relieved of his duties. I applied for conscientious objector status but was denied because I was already twenty-two and had not applied at my eighteenth birthday.

All that time I did everything in school but finish my degree. I took courses in creative writing, in film and photography, always thinking that each semester would be my last. And when at last the lottery was set up and my number was thirty-six, I knew that the semester I was in would be my last. By then I also knew I was against the war and could never serve in any conventional way.

I went to Michigan one weekend and told my father I was either going to go to jail or move to Canada. He said he couldn't agree with either alternative. He told me to "suck in my pride" and go, just go to war, like everybody else. They would see I was smart, I had bad eyesight, I could speak other languages. They would never put me in the front lines. My father had been turned away from serving in World War II because of a bad back and bad feet, which necessitated steel arch supports. The war he missed made him more of a patriot than if he had served. He was a hawk, I was a dove, and no matter how long we talked, we were always going to be these different birds.

It was one of the few times I ever talked about "the issues" with my father. He was a Republican, conservative on every issue. He blamed college for the discrepancy between us. "All that schooling made you too damn smart for your own good," he said once. We avoided politics in any conversation, except for occasional quips he made about Democratic presidents when they got into predicaments, and then he would blame my vote for putting them in the presidency by saying, "Your boy Kennedy really did it this time" or "Your boy Jimmy really blew it on that one."

I wanted him to say he would support whatever decision I made, but he couldn't bring himself to say that. And then I found a way out, a compromise we could both live with. I agreed to go to the Far East to teach college-level English courses on military bases for the University of Maryland, the one stipulation, and the reason there were still openings, being a commitment to go to Vietnam as well as Japan, Korea, Taiwan, Okinawa, and Thailand. I went without the blessings of my local draft board.

And so I finally went to Vietnam in 1970. I may have been the only one in all those crazy years who went to Vietnam (as a civilian teacher) to avoid going there (as a soldier). To me, the distinction was a matter of conscientious objection. I could continue being an American, without having to go to jail, move to Canada, or carry weapons in the war. I have been "returning" ever since.

My Vietnam is a pathology of smells I can never forget. I step off my World Airways flight in Saigon and gasp for air. Saigon is steamy wet with heat. People and baggage shimmer from the blur of spent fuel in the air. I walk from the plane into the terminal, and I am drenched with sweat, a sweat so fast and frightening there is almost no smell to it. My shoes are uncomfortably hot, as though Western leather was never meant to be worn here.

The terminal at Ton Son Nhut is a city unto itself. Soldiers are everywhere, standing in long MAC lines, sitting on benches, or stretched out on the floor, all wearing sunglasses, many with boom boxes, all in green and black fatigues. They are both American and Vietnamese. The Americans look sloppy, their sleeves rolled up, a tattoo showing, a box of Marlboros tucked in the fold of sleeve, an occasional earring, beret, or cowboy hat. They smell tacky with sweat, good things gone bad, like greasy french fries on the boardwalks back home. The Vietnamese, on the other hand, look trumped-up, like toy soldiers, rigid as a railroad. They do not mingle with the Americans. They do not mingle with the women in the airport. They sit alone and brood, like statuary.

They are all in transit. They are all mercenaries. They all look bored and mean.

I smell fruit before I see the women selling fruit: bruised mangoes, dates wet and live with flies, soft kiwi like some voodoo parody of shrunken monkey skulls, and runt bananas, yellow fingers that refuse to curl. The women talk nonstop, even when they have no customers. They whine when they talk. I can see the red stains on their teeth from the betel nuts they chew. I can smell vinegar and cabbage on their breath. When I get too close to them, they are selling more than fruit. They offer hash, Saigon tea, porcelain elephants, black-market watches and radios, fucking or sucking, all in the same breath, all public, no sense of hierarchy, priority, value, or transgression.

They, too, are in transit. All mercenaries. They all look bored and mean. They have breasts, but their breasts don't give me longing. They give me a fright, a fear of being white.

I have made a terrible mistake. I have come to Vietnam with the naive and vulgar belief that I can be a tourist here, a civilian who can escape the military, a traveler who can speak French, smoke Gitane cigarettes, eat *pain au chocolat*, drink espresso, and read *Le Monde* in the morning.

I want to treat Saigon like the south of France and my stay here as that of some kind of journalist on extended assignment. I am separated from the woman I have asked to marry me. She is teaching in Louisiana, where they speak Creole French, I am teaching in Saigon where they speak another kind of French, and we are both on extended assignment, on hold, until we can both go back to graduate school and be who we were before. I choose not to see the USO, with crippled children begging for piastres around the door. I choose not to see the endless open bars with no doors, in which the GIs buy watered-down Saigon tea, their backs to the bar, sitting on stools with their legs spread, and the bar girls walk into them, between the lock of their legs, giving kisses, promising more, bringing drinks that have not been ordered. I choose not to see the gaudy velvet sheen of street-corner art, a Day-Glo stoned Jesus on the cross with the inscription on the cross: KILL GOOKS. I choose not to see every American infection of a local economy spaced out and gone rotten. Instead, I smell baguettes in a bakery on Tudo Street. I hear French spoken at the Continental Hotel. I buy a pack of blue Gauloise cigarettes and a bottle of Châteauneuf-du-Pape, and I pretend I am back on the cobblestone streets in Aix-en-Provence.

And suddenly, my first afternoon in Saigon, I realize I have walked some thirty streets without stopping, refusing to barter, refusing to buy. I have tried to walk myself into an invisibility that would protect me from the forced contact of strangers, the frantic despair, the growing swell of crowds gone bullish and mad. I am no longer a boy, no longer a Catholic or language major or liberal Democrat. My conscientious objection to the war holds no currency here. I am just a fool.

And if I am a fool, then I am just as dangerous or endangered as the fanatics I presume to oppose. Off-kilter, out of sync, arbitrarily made horrorful. I have a chill. It is over one hundred degrees, the open sewers are clogged, and I shake if I stand still. I walk and am foolish.

I go to my temporary billeting, a room at the New Vietnam Hotel, where the sheets are white and wet, the blades of the fan overhead are noisy and offer no breeze, and the water from the tap is reddish brown like blood. I lie down and the maid comes. The bed is already made and I sit up, wondering why she has come in my room, holding her shoes in her hand, smiling, her teeth crooked and missing and stained. She seems to recognize me. I am the *other*, the American other, and she smiles at me, comes closer to me than strangers should come, and smiles the way blackjack dealers hail a mark.

She undoes two buttons of her blouse and pulls her left breast out of the cup of her bra. She looks at it, then at me looking at it. She pinches something, maybe a flea or chigger, squeezes it, and flicks it into the air. She tweaks her nipple and it responds, instantly erect.

"You want, honey?" she asks, and her breath upon me is almost enough to make me gag.

"Non, merci," I say, still trying to refuse this country as a Frenchman in order not to be found out as some ugly American.

"I clean. You no worry."

"I'm sure you are," I say, pointing to the bed and room, as though they were proof of her hygiene, "but I just got here and I'm pretty dirty."

I have been raised to be polite this way: to put the responsibility for all refusals upon myself and not on others.

"I like dirty okay plenty fine, too," she says, grinning widely now, so that I suddenly see her age more clearly as somewhere between twelve and fifteen. "I let you do me anywhere."

"Please," I plead.

I do not trust that I can make her leave with words, so I get up and go into the bathroom, closing the door behind me. I wait there for twenty minutes, until I am reasonably sure she has gone. When she has gone, I laugh, begin to chain-smoke and talk to myself. I have come over ten thousand miles to lock myself in a bathroom, in fear of the child *mamasan* who makes my bed.

I go to dinner in the hotel restaurant, and I think I have over-reacted. I eat with American soldiers, all officers, all TDY, which is the designation for "temporary duty." One is a B52 pilot from Utapao in Thailand. Another flies the C130s out of Kadena Air Base on Okinawa. Another is a systems analyst from Pusan, Korea. Yet they are all in Saigon. I ask them why, and they laugh at me. Technically, Richard Nixon has begun the process of troop reduction and withdrawal. It is still being called reduction, not yet retreat. But through TDY deployment the troop size swells, even as the official count shrinks.

These men are full of the war, full of stories about strikes, prostitutes, the latest purchase, their R&R plans, the telling of which I inhibit by the simple fact that I am a civilian, an "outsider." They are heavy drinkers, casual braggarts, quick in their repartee and camaraderie, fierce in their feelings, and united in their hatred of everything Vietnamese. But they do not know how to have me at their table. They are resentful of my GS-13 rank, which gives me officer status, especially when I have long hair, wear blue jeans, and carry no gun. They do not see that I am at risk too.

They dare not ask questions that will remind them of their loved ones back home, but they are curious, and so they ask me questions in a general way "about the world." Are the Cleveland Browns a good team this year? How about earthquakes in California? Was there enough snow to ski the past winter? Who is hot and who is not in rock and roll? They seem disappointed with my answers.

Dessert is a runny flan pudding, white rice on brown custard, that the men joke about instead of eating. They call the rice "white boogers." They hurry through coffee, which sobers them enough to get up from the table. They go to the lounge to watch television, a rebroadcast of a football game played the week before. The game is in Green Bay, one of them says. I wonder why this is important. Max, the B52 pilot from Utapao, stays behind with me. He seems to be reading my mind.

"They don't just want to see the game," he says. "They know the score already from *Stars and Stripes*. They want to see it snow. I can't get into that kind of homesickness."

It never snows in Vietnam. Snow, American snow, remains pure, as undefiled as apple pie and memories of Mom. They will huddle together in the lounge, sweating in short sleeves, drinking warm beer, rooting for one team or the other, but more interested in falling snow than in the final score.

"How do they know there'll be snow?"

"Final score was six to three," he says. "Had to be snowing."

"You want my dessert?" I ask.

"No way. Never eat the dessert. Gives you the runs. Why did you say you were here?"

"I told you. I'm a teacher."

"So you said. Teaching's the last thing I'd figure over here. Just crazy enough to make you CIA, though. Don't suppose you'd tell me if you were."

"I'm not CIA."

"You married?"

"Not yet. Are you?"

"Why I'm here. To stay married. If I was home, we'd be getting divorced and she'd be sitting on half."

"Is that the only reason?"

"You wouldn't understand the others."

"Try me."

"Okay. I get a certain satisfaction out of flying my bird, going a long distance, dropping my crate of eggs and getting back to base without a scratch. I get a certain satisfaction knowing that the landscape's been changed once and for all time after I've been there. I couldn't ever get that back in the world flying commercial. You need a war to get that kind of clarity. As long as there's a war, I can get my kind of kick. I told you you wouldn't understand."

"It has to do with passion."

"More like precision. Control. And maybe a bit of playing God in the clouds. Passion, if you like, of a maximum sort."

He leaves me with flushed cheeks, him swirling on unsteady feet in the air, me grounded at the table, eggs dropped on target. I think I see his satisfaction as a rouge upon his face, something ruddy with jaws agape, live lobsters spanking wet out of the net. I think he thought he had put me in my peacenik place, humiliated me with the facts of life, and now he was free to watch football with his buddies, while I carried the half-life of his actions like a scar.

I go outside, to the mobs of people going back and forth, as though their sole role in life, like whole cities in Mexico after siesta and before supper, were to go back and forth, amble, mill, push, hover, shove, be elbows and breath and underarms. Impossible not to be touched, shoved, crowded, and swept without going into the street, the frenzy of mopeds and bikes and military jeeps, or going back inside, literally disappearing into one's room and the loss of ego waiting there.

A man knocks me to the side, and I am pushed to the right. Something goes by my left ear, the whistle of it staying in my ear, like water whistling after swimming laps. The something is a bullet, heard but not seen. It goes through the back of the head of the man in front of me, and he collapses, which collapse seems impossible in this coerced crowd flow. I actually step on him, trip over the body, stumbling, getting up and turning around to apologize, when I notice he has not gotten up. The Vietnamese man is dead, his hair matted with blood like an old paintbrush stiff with tint and never turpentined. The ARVN police, two of them with guns drawn, in their gray uniforms and conical white caps, their heads shaped like silly silver bullets, the police referred to by Americans as the "white mice," stand over the body of the man, ready to fire again if he moves. He doesn't move. Finally, one of the white mice turns the body over with a kick of his foot. The baguette of bread is there in both clutched hands, crushed, flattened, the shreds of crust like sawdust.

The American MPs arrive in their jeep, yelling in English, "Clear the area." One of the white mice explains in smattered English.

"He is thief. Bread stole."

An inversion of words. No call, no warning shot, no reading of rights. The flattened baguette, becoming thick and gummy with human blood, no good to anyone now, punishable by death.

I do not realize immediately how close I have come to the same bullet going through my head, if not for the thief jostling me, pushing me aside. I feel guilt. I think he has saved my life and I have repaid him by stepping on his fallen body, somehow causing his death as much as if I had shot him myself.

I am in shock and shaking. One of the American MPs notices me, sees I am an American, a civilian who shakes.

"You saw?"

I nod but cannot speak.

"Get off the street," he says in a whisper. "People get the wrong idea, seeing a civilian standing around a body."

He doesn't ask my name or where I am staying. He doesn't say I will be called in later for questioning. There is no attempt to secure witnesses. Already the white mice have piled the body into the back of the jeep, where his arms hang over the back, as though he had died there and not on the sidewalk.

I go back to my room and lie on the bed, totally dressed, still shaking, my eyes on the blades of the fan. I don't know when I close my eyes and fall asleep. I only know that the sentence comes to me, as though dictated: "I am TDY from my senses."

How strange. Everyone looks like Van Gogh without the ear, both American and Vietnamese: the wide eyes of somnambulists, long toothed, the fidgeting gestures, the haughty demeanor of those who've walked the fiery coals.

Thus ends my first full day in Vietnam. In the morning I receive a letter from my local draft board, forwarded by my parents in Michigan. I have been drafted. I am to be inducted. I am supposed to report to a center in Detroit on a given date.

I am already here.

Let them come and get me.

This is the first of seven notices I am to receive during my two years in the Far East. I throw them all away. I dare to laugh at them. I have skipped all the steps. I am already here. What can they threaten me with? Jail? No one would stand for it. Jail is for those who refuse to go. Not only did I not refuse to go, but I have come here *before* they told me to. They cannot punish what precedes their laws.

The local draft board in Michigan is enraged. I have become

a scandal for them. They cannot *not* draft me, but nor can they succeed in getting the deed done. I still wear civilian clothes, even at the height of Tet, but I do not carry a gun and cannot be made to kill anyone. I have found a way to serve my country without disserving myself. The secretary of the local draft board continues to send induction notices, and her anger is expressed in the fact that the lowercase letters have all gone to caps, as though she were dealing with a myopic.

A terrible and perverse freedom dawns on me. I cannot go home, of course. Nor can I fit into the war around me. I have come in naive desperation, only to be stripped of all appearance at the airport. I am in every way ugly, hideous, here but not here, against the war but kept alive by the military presence that perpetuates the war. Finally, I am no one, living nowhere. Only a fake APO address in San Francisco can find me. I am here in Vietnam but not counted as being here. I am totally TDY. I can even cut my own orders, fly to Australia if I want to, and no one will stop me. A civilian with orders of his own cutting is more to be feared than a general.

I fly by chopper to classes in Quonset huts at Bien Hoa and other classes in log cabins at Long Binh, surrounded by red clay that could be Georgia, if there were only pine trees around. There are no trees in Saigon, there are no trees at either of these bases, and so I look down longingly at treetops in the distances between these bases.

Sometimes, the women who work for the Red Cross fly the choppers with us. They serve coffee and doughnuts at the bases. If they're attractive, the men call them "donut dollies"; if they're not attractive, they're called "pastry pigs." I can't tell the difference. They all look tough and battle hardened to me. They look like they were born in the 1930s: hair coiled in bouffant; faces layered in lipstick, always dried and a little caked in this heat; rouge and mascara in war-zone off-colors, pastels of pink or lilac; accusatory bullet bras, always at stiff and limited attention; aggressive hands. If they are pretty enough, I am "bumped" off the chopper.

"No class tonight, doc," the chopper pilot tells me on the wind-swept pad. "Too much T and A for cargo."

One of my students at Bien Hoa dies at Russian roulette. Another student at Long Binh dies of a heroin overdose. Both are listed as battle casualties and shipped home. I am told to give them a grade of Incomplete, which will become part of their permanent service record.

At Cam Ranh Bay there are no official latrines for the Viet-namese *mamasans* who clean the hutches, so they urinate and defecate in the bunkers. All the men know this, so when the siren alert announces "incoming" and the base is under rocket attack, nobody goes to the bunkers. I give a final exam at Cam Ranh Bay during one of those rocket attacks. The students are all on the floor underneath their desks, laughing at the absurdity of taking a final exam under such conditions. Nobody takes me seriously when I tell them there will be no makeup exam. The walls vibrate, the lights go out, and finally part of the ceiling comes down.

Half the class leaves en masse, M16s in hand, glad in a giddy way that the war has interrupted their final exam. The other half stays, but they are too distracted to write another line. They clock time: look at me, look at each other, as though they were waiting for a signal to bolt. Most of them are probably stoned.

I remember Vietnam as a function of having survived it: mo-ments girded with caution and radically separated from other mo-ments, whose passion is only apparent years later by virtue of memory, the latent reflex of memory almost lazy with shock.

I remember playing basketball on the beaches at Nha Trang, my students and I, all of us naked or nearly so, sweating and sparkling with sand and salt spray, hurting with sunburn, with baskets made of concertina wire that sooner or later will puncture the ball. I remember hand-feeding strawberries to a prostitute who asked me to teach her about Catholicism. And I remember the monsoons at Tet, rain thicker than a trenchcoat, threatening to drown both sides of the war in mud, and how we used to endure the monsoons in the BOQs by playing our music as loud as we could play it—Hendrix or Doors or whatever was at hand—because we knew nobody would complain. And I remember crossing the street to get out of the way of black soldiers who had gone AWOL in Saigon and who lived in Soul Alley: men in fatigues and dashikis with machine guns and two or three Vietnamese women as entourage.

I don't remember seeing a single bird in Vietnam. Maybe the skies were too noisy and overcrowded with metal things, chopper blades, falling bombs, and wind shear. Maybe the trees were missing or maimed or defoliated with chemicals. Maybe the few remaining fool birds were killed for food. I don't finally know the reason why, but I never saw a single bird.

I wrote home and told them I was happy. I lied in all my letters.

On my bird out of Saigon for Tokyo, I actually cried, because my father the hawk had become a dove for me. The obsession with the local draft board was over. I had four brothers, all draft eligible, and none of them ever received a single induction notice.

Michigan

Everyone knows that Michigan presents itself as a hand: specifically, the inside of a right hand, thumb to the east. Michiganders don't hold up a hand to show where they come from when talking to other Michiganders, but to everyone else, yes, the hand goes up, the other hand serves as a pointer, to say, "I come from there." I knew from a very early age, for example, that my father's "people" were farmers who came from the thumb, even though I had never been to the thumb, had no prospects of going to the thumb, and imagined that region, not as a digit, but as the water that surrounded it. And it's the water, the awareness of water, that has stayed with me, even though I haven't lived in Michigan for over twenty-five years. My affinity for coastal states—Maine, North Carolina, Florida, California— has to do with recognizing Michigan in them, whole patches of my childhood, always surrounded by water, and not the Great Lakes, which define Michigan for people from other states, those Great Lakes (we learned them by the acronym *home*) for which I can only muster an occasional curiosity of accidental tourism but certainly no pride of ownership. The water awareness I grew up with came from the bays and inland lakes, the thousand hidden sprawls of lakes that stemmed from the middle of the hand up through the fingers.

If I begin with the figure of the hand, I do so to point out that by some sleight of hand, the reasons for which are still elusive, Michigan moved after I grew up. When I was a child, Michigan was still the Midwest, a core state of a broader Midwest that included all those other states whose schools belonged to the Big Ten. The East, South, and Midwest were well defined; the West was nebulous at best. Kansas and Nebraska were the West; California and Oregon were the Far West. I'm tempted to call this cowboy geography now, the West referring to our mythical past of seemingly endless frontiers and rough-tough territories, a geography of ignorance and hope, states "out there," defined more by what they were *not* than by what they were.

I grew up thinking Michigan was an integral part of the Midwest, and that thinking was reinforced in the schools. We were told that Michigan supplied cars to the world, that we had the best highways and road repair system in the country, that our farms were bountiful, our schools were effective, and our lifestyle was the envy of many other states in the country. We were told we spoke "midwestern English," which was equated with Standard English. We couldn't have felt more American.

Somewhere along the line, Kansas and Nebraska became the new Midwest, and Michigan was relegated to far North status: too cold, too isolated, too dependent on the troubled steel and automotive industries. What brought about this shift in geography? Maybe what I have called a cowboy geography was in reality an outdated cartography, overly influenced by the Civil War: specifically, the limits of how far west that war extended. Maybe there was an arrogant chauvinism attached to Detroit's former monopoly of the automotive industry that skewed its sense of geography. More likely, the increased mobility of Americans, reapportioned political representation among the states, and the enormous influence of television have conspired to shift our sense of geography. Whatever the reasons, Michigan has been impounded like a stray dog, overlooked at the federal level, even at a time when the state could finally boast of its first president (Gerald Ford), cast adrift by its lack of diversity in industry, brokered and leased, sold and resold, bankrupt and aching. When I was a boy, I took pride in the fact that Hemingway's early stories were Michigan stories, that in George Romney we had the farthest-from-Utah Mormon governor. Even our shame was our pride: for example, Al Capone vacationing at the Grand Hotel on Mackinac Island. Now the notoriety of Michigan comes from a film like *Roger and Me* and certain national publications declaring Flint, Muskegon, and Grand Rapids among the worst places in the country to live. More personally, I have watched my father, a lifelong Michigan resident, abdicate his domain, moving to Florida, moving his residency there, becoming one of the thousands of "snowbirds," (those migratory white-haired pilgrims who winter in Florida and summer in Michigan, Ohio, Indiana). He declared proudly, a bit too vehemently for my understanding, that he would never shovel snow again.

Ironically, at a time when others are moving out of the state, I have reached a point in my life (mid-forties, midlife) where I can no longer repress my Michigan roots, where I can finally embrace the importance of that place in my psyche, where I am compelled to go back again and again, the opposite odyssey of that of my father. He doesn't understand this at all. I am only beginning to.

Ten years ago, I began single-parenting three sons, who were at that time four, two, and one. I barely made it through that year of teaching in Pennsylvania and decided I couldn't face a summer alone, without family or support group around me, so I resolved, more out of despair than anything else, to pack the car and take my babies to Michigan, and there to expose my children to my brothers and sisters, to put them together with my widower-father at the cottage on the lake, and, quite frankly, to stay there as long as I possibly could, until I was asked to leave. It was all well and good and even noble to justify my trip by thinking that I was giving my children extended family, that I was letting my children see people who looked and talked and acted like me, to give them a grandfather at a time when separation had deprived them of their mother and, to some extent, her mother and father, and death had deprived them of my mother. My father seemed to me that first summer as a formidable *ancestor*, the keeper of the past, he who held the family stories and secrets.

Of course, it didn't work out that way. After a brief novelty period, my father withdrew into his Parkinson's, and he became too remote for my sons to stay interested. Both my father and my sons relied on me to be the buffer, the carrier of conversation, the cook and bottle washer. More and more, my sons left the cottage early in the morning and came back only for meals. They fished and swam, found frogs and crayfish, skipped stones and took walks. Their city ways sloughed off, and the three of them acted like little Tom Sawyers/Huck Finns. We stopped rolling up the car windows and locking the doors. I stopped feeling for my billfold when someone bumped into me at the grocery store. My boys laughed and splashed their way through countless sunny days on the blue lake, surrounded by birch trees, bending willows, and the piano-key tinkling of poplars at their tops. The smell of weeds and fish aroused them. I stood at the screen door, still vaguely listening to my father talk about the Detroit Tigers, watching my boys grow visibly taller, taller and leaner, shedding their winter fat. Their tanned bodies and healthy appetites ("everything tastes good at the cottage, even peas") were proof that I had done the right thing. In the slow sameness of the days, like beads on a rosary, I seemed to be feeling new hope and strength. And when my boys finally complained about the boredom of our days there, the complaints were mild and mixed with the awareness of the pain we had come from, the hard days we would soon return to.

Each summer after that one, my boys and I talked about longer and more ambitious trips, a "roughing it" trip through Montana and Wyoming, a drive through the desert to California, a swing to the Southwest. But each time we got to the cottage on the lake, we knew we were there to stay, and not just because of the relatives, the familiarity, or the "free stays." My sons appreciate the ritual of these trips, anticipate a year's worth of memories, race to get to the first fishing, first swimming, first run around the lake. And I appreciate that what used to be my memories from my childhood are now either completed or gone or subsumed by *our* memories, our cumulative ten-year commitment to going there.

It has taken me the full ten years of going there to realize that the renewed hope and strength I was feeling every month of July to be there came from the place more than from the people. At first, I assumed that "place" referred very particularly to the cottage outside Farwell, Michigan, a cottage built by my father as a gift to my mother at my sister's birth, the cottage where I lived every summer as a boy, swimming and fishing, chasing frogs and playing baseball. But gradually I realized that the "place" was as wide as the state itself and included roads not taken, unseen cities, and unswum lakes. Some nights at the lake, my boys safely asleep in their beds, I have gotten in my car to drive, no destination in mind, just to feel the chilly night air, thick with fog and pine scent, passing the farms where the people slept invisibly and the

animals stood in black silhouette against the moonscape like statuary, listening to the lonesome trains running parallel to the roads
I drove, feeling neither young nor old but somewhere in between,
neither happy nor sad but a melancholy in between.

Slowly, over time, the landscape I had known and trusted as
a child has suffered from erosion. The small towns, with their
faded postcards (still five cents), their ceiling fans and creaking
floorboards, were giving way to the K Mart and fast-food chains.
But I ignored them. I looked instead at the all-night diners, small
and crowded with truckers with tattoos, the Amish tents where by
day they sold their quilts and plates, the "local" and in-between
places.

Slowly, over time, I have had to acknowledge some changes. I
no longer know if a farm is prosperous or not. The wide sprawl of
flat land is there, the rows of corn are still there, the smell of fertil-
izer is still pungent, but the silo is now obscured by a satellite dish,
the John Deere tractor is now in a shed or on the front lawn with
a FOR SALE sign on it. People in Michigan still buy only American
cars, those big "boats" of cars (Broughams, Bonnevilles, Skylarks),
but many of them have FOR SALE signs as well. The gas stations
along the less-traveled roads still advertise for fishing supplies, live
bait, sometimes even guns and ammo, but they also sell videos.
Yard sales are epidemic. Jobs are scarce. Country-western music
seems to be the sound of choice, from the middle of the state up to
Canada. There are still more baseball fields than churches; even
the smallest towns have two or three baseball fields, often back-to-
back, but the outfields are hard and parched, piebald in their lack
of grass, while the football stadiums, when the city is large enough
to warrant one, are new, well kept, even in summer. Everyone
seems to own a boat (from cabin cruisers to pontoons to sleek black
speed merchants that look like Stealth bombers), but they're more

often in the yard with the familiar FOR SALE sign than in the water. Each summer now, there is a new scandal about dumping in the Saginaw Bay or at Tawas, industrial waste or fecal coliform, with the result that the state parks close, the beaches are empty, the boats stay docked at the marinas.

The whole state seems heavy with pause, overextended, up for grabs. A so-called buyer's market, if buyers could be induced to come. My favorite birches are soot smudged with disease, besieged by gypsy moths. The churches take on a Spanish look, many-angled as a hacienda, with curved tile rooftops, glittering crosses, and ever-more-byzantine stained-glass depictions, so that the Stations of the Cross look cubist. These churches are filled with old people, praying for the young who've gone. The original Main Streets of cities, the old downtowns, those places built around the rivers, feel eerie in their abandonment, poignant in their pathetic attempts to bring people back from the suburbs and malls through parades, rebates, and giveaways of houses, cars, and boats. The urban centers look like movie lots for nostalgia films, while the margin of the suburbs, always extending the sameness of houses and trees, forcibly swallows the farms and dirt roads, all those *in-between* places I loved so much. The tragedy of all this slippage into so-called progress is muted by the cleanliness, the lack of rust and rubble and graffiti we associate with decay. There is still a brisk tourist traffic in summer, transforming I-75 and old 27 into slow bumper-to-bumper caravans, remindful of the roads in southern Florida. The lakes are still there in Gaylord and Grayling, Au Gres and Cadillac, even though the fish population seems to have changed drastically, from perch based to pike and bass, and these latter less frequent, more battle wise. The cherry trees still sparkle with bings at Traverse City, famous for its asylum and regatta, and the Mexicans still migrate from Texas and Oklahoma to pick, but the markets are not as plentiful, the weather and birds grow more inimical, and crop failures are as common as sparrows.

I notice all these things, notice them with a crispness and awareness of contour that only professional photographers are supposed to have. I notice them all the more acutely as I grow older. I have never lived in a place I loved, a place that nurtured me. I have always had to live where the work was. I stand on the varnished dock boards at the lake, wearing my father's baseball caps, feeling the lazy stubble of beard and mustache on my face, staring intently, as though there were some hidden secret in the fishbowl sky, some eureka of insight to be gained in watching bass break water, some clarity or resolution to the longing in my lungs. But no, there is only this beautiful staring. The marvel of this place is that it remains impersonal in its beauty, does not care a damn for me, will not let me work or resettle, will only accommodate me partially.

I am famous for my tunnel vision, my apparent unawareness of my surroundings, the dirty baseboards in my apartment, the piles of papers that fill every available corner, books piled on books, and pictures of my children on top of those piles. As a writer, I have always known that my weakness was setting, the quick lip service I have paid to place. I seem to be able to work and live in polluted cities, oblivious to the lack of sun and water around me.

All of this seems to be changing, slowly and over time, as I recognize that place is important; that place houses memories every bit as much as the mind; that place, in fact, is an extension of the body. I used to think that poets able to remember the names of flowers were a precious lot. As I begin to garden, I no longer think that way. My sense of place is becoming as acute as my sense of smell. I have always had strange premonitions about places, feelings I couldn't explain, as mysterious as prejudice and irrational numbers. I spent time teaching in Vietnam, and as long as I was in Cam Ranh Bay or Bien Hoa or Saigon, I knew I was "safe"; but if I ever dared to go to Da Nang, I felt I would die there. I spent a year in Madrid on a Fulbright and never once felt it was home. I spent one day in Dublin and felt instantly that it could be home. South America has always intrigued me, but Africa not at all. The flatness of the Midwest that so benumbs East Coast and West Coast drivers relaxes me, is balm to my eyes. The red clay and loblolly pines of South Georgia seem "menacing" to many northerners, as though the woods were full of poisonous snakes and redneck hunters, but to me they are poetic, alive, otherworldly. The vast desolate spaces between towns in Texas put off some people, give them a longing for miniature, but to me they are the stuff and substance of that state, where I want to be when I'm there, not in the glass elevators of downtown Houston or the grassy knoll in Dallas. Much like a finicky eater cannot explain his or her likes and dislikes, I have been drawn to places and repulsed by places, both irrationally and in my stomach, as though some were filet mignon and others were rancid liver and overfried onions.

How do places speak to us this way? They seem to hold invisible "remotes," to toggle our memories, change our channels, play the body like a piano. Perhaps this last simile can be elided: places play the body, period. The body is the piano; the mind, then, becomes both the sheet music that precedes the playing and the sound of the piano playing. The way that tea with madeleine was a trigger for memory in Proust, the way that smells of food, the sound of music, and sensorial data "play" us (interesting aside: the more direct senses—the visual and tactile—are less effective memory triggers than the more indirect—the aural and olfactory), so too places can surround the body with immediacy and urgency, the senses booted up with extra megs of memory and déjà vu.

Places that affect us this powerfully cease to be mere spaces, areas of length and width and depth. They become temporal, to carry with them such a mental rush. They are, in fact, our particular coordinates, as well as our limits, of space-time. Put me in Montreal or Mexico City and I am a perfectly rational tourist, empowered by fluency in French and Spanish, able to get along quite nicely in both places. Put me back in Michigan and my heart speeds up, my reflexes slow down, and I begin to swallow the sights until I am bloated. There is time in the tinkling atop the poplars, time in the bow-and-arrow bend of the birches, time in the rake-teeth look of the rippling lake, the sound of boats banging against dock boards like honking geese, the sound of The Doors or Frank Sinatra from the bonfires across the lake. And there is time as well inside the cottage: time in all the old *Redbook* magazines my mother bought in the fifties, stacked in the clothes hamper in the bathroom; time in the peephole in the knotty pine, from which my brothers and I used to stare into the bathroom (the hole is still there, but we have grown too big to get up to it through the small walk-up into the attic); time in the mood barometer my mother always kept pointed at "crabby," unless it was my father's birthday, and then it would shift for a day to "loving"; time in the damp, musky bedsheets, off-white and worn thin as communion wafers over time. No deck of cards has ever been thrown away at the cottage. "I'll Be Loving You," "You Were Meant for Me," and "Always" are still inside the piano bench, yellow eared but still very playable. The Frank Yerby novels my mother used to read for thrills and private fantasies are still there on the top shelf.

She has been dead ten years now, my mother. In those first two or three years after her death, my father used to sit in his black felt recliner and wait for her to come back. Not consciously, according to him, but suddenly, abruptly. He would come out of an afternoon nap violently, having heard a car door slam or a screen door close. And he would wait for my mother to come in, mix of excitement at the prospect and anger. Yes, anger. He was going to scold her for being away so long. Were she to come back, she would find the cottage more or less as she left it, time trapped in that place as though a vault had been shut around it.

My mother used to say that couples who had been married a long time began to look alike. Pressed for more details, she used to say that it didn't matter whether the two people loved each other or not (it probably helped if they did); it just mattered that they stayed together *a long time*. Longevity was the key. And maybe longevity is also the key to the power of place on a changing body. As a boy in Michigan, I experienced all of the things described here so much more directly than now, but I never thought to hold them, save them, savor them. I never thought "this time" or "next time" or "maybe for the last time"; I never thought time, except to hurry into my future where I was already a professional baseball player, photographer, and stunt pilot (bad eyesight ruined my chances at all three). Thirty-some years later, I experience these things in a mediated way, less directly but more deeply. I am acutely aware of my own mortality (shortness of breath, receding hairline, lapses in memory, a sudden need of bifocals, and so on), and the lie I feel as truth is that my favorite places are also mortal. I experience them as body. I want to make love to this body again and again before it goes. A way of not having to say "before I go."

Ten years of summer trips to Michigan have been monster successes for my children. They are more than context or backdrop or poor man's holiday. They are more than family tree and a need for ritual. Each year my sons say that they are too big now to go back to Michigan. Now that they are teenagers, they know the cottage for the musky, unkempt place that it is; they see the blight of trees and feel no poetry; they sense the fish have gotten smaller as they have gotten bigger. They are no longer in thrall of my car stories, they complain that my pitching has slowed down to "junk," they have long ago stopped feeling every highway stop with a primary narcissism that interprets the stop as a private gift. In short, I have become their scapegoat for all the wrong turns, hot weather, and flat farm fields. They stay in the car and complain bitterly when I stop for yard sales. And yet, once we are there, they are too busy to help me unpack. They run to the water, regress in their skin, and have the time of their lives.

I have two memories: one real, one imagined. The real one is not situated in a given time; it could have happened any summer among some fifteen or twenty summers. I am in the back seat of the car my mother is driving. I am sitting next to a box of mason jars that hold the canned jams my mother made in the winter months. My mother is answering the umpteenth question of "When will we be there?" from any one or all of her seven children. I can hear her gum smacking as she drives. She drives too slowly, the car full of kids, long before the days of seat belts. Little town after little town, she wants to stop for roadside sales. There is fresh sweet corn, raspberries or strawberries, homegrown tomatoes. We threaten her with bickering among ourselves if she dares to stop. And just when we are about to give up hope, half of us have to go to the bathroom badly, the asphalt gives way to dirt, the breezes whip up and swirl through the car, the sound of the waterfall at the dam can be heard. And when we pull into the dirt driveway to the cottage, we bolt. She begs for help with the unpacking. We make promises to help, but we don't mean them. We bolt. Last one to the lake is a rotten . . . Hours later, when some of us remember that we *still* have to go to the bathroom and others feel suddenly hungry, we go up to the cottage in groups, never one by one, and there we find sandwiches already made, sitting on plates and waiting for us, as though they had been there all winter long.

The imagined memory I have is this: one day, when my father is gone and I am gone, my sons will come back to Michigan, either singly or as a group, perhaps to have a reunion there. Maybe the cottage is still there, maybe not, but one thing is certain: they will seek out water, one of the many lakes. They will wear baseball caps and stop shaving for days. They will say the food tastes great, whatever it is, and they will wonder who I was to them, why I took them here. They will tell horror stories of our trips, voice-over for a highlights film. And they will intuit, even if they have no words for it, that this place has something to do with their bodies, with moving through the body, with loneliness in the pit of beauty, with learning how to cope with loneliness.

And anything I might have left them in my will will pale next to this moment.

Indiana

There are certain small towns in the Midwest that threaten coastal dwellers (New Yorkers, southern Californians) so much that they would rather fly across country and never see these towns by car or, God forbid, on foot. For such people, these towns represent a stereotype of exclusion: towns flanked by flat highways and farm fields, towns that announce their cleanliness with Chamber of Commerce WELCOME signs, that proclaim their old-fashioned values by their many churches. They are assumed to lack crime as well as vitality and nightlife. They are assumed to uphold family values, even as they are suspicious of strangers and diversity. They are called by many names: the Heartland, the wheat belt, the flatlands. The cursory glance tells all: there is no Hard Rock Cafe here, no stand-up comedy clubs, no good deli food, no Bloomingdales, no all-night jazz, no City Lights bookstores. There must be, then, what? Well, a ton of boredom. Listening to the cows low on balmy summer nights. Fanatical high school sports programs. Outdoor church suppers, Bingo nights, 4H clubs, mashed potatoes and gravy, Christians, old folks, bib jeans, country-western music stations, yard sales. A ton of boredom. Put four to the floor.

But these very same things, including all the stereotypes just mentioned, speak to the souls of some people. Returning to them is a return to childhood memories, rites of passage that stay unmolested by a slowly changing landscape, a return to belonging to a clan or community not found in Manhattan or Los Angeles, no matter how long one has lived in those places as a transplant. There are few converts either way, and maybe you need to have been born to it, but the boredom felt by others is a timelessness to me, a poetic melancholy, a place to lie down and take stock of dreams.

I would never have discovered southern Indiana if I hadn't gone to graduate school there, Indiana University at Bloomington. I had grown up in Michigan and had gone to undergraduate school in Ann Arbor, so I was still in the Big Ten, still in a neighboring state, so how different could it be? Well, like night and day. Southern Indiana is more "southern" than many places south of it. Bloomington may present a facade of classic values and clean streets and uniform limestone buildings, but the satellite sites, like Seymour, Bean Blossom, Gnaw Bone, and the like, were filled with hunker-down hootenannies, fiddlers and carpenters, clay makers and potters, artists and artisans, country bumpkins and gentlemen farmers, hippies and stonecutters. To drive out of Bloomington was to drive out of education, out of the safe sterility of a progressive city and into timelessness, people who had dropped out, were hiding out, were going back to the land, communes and loners coexisting in the woods. Films like *Breaking Away* and *Hoosiers* present the twang of Indiana speech, the innocence of growing up, and old-fashioned heroism, Heartland-style. And while there is the Little 500 and Bobby Knight basketball to back up such films' truth claims, the diversity has been edited out. The films lack black people, Chinese, and Lebanese. They show the limestone quarries but not all the back-to-nature, bare-naked swimming that went on there, casually, sometimes almost religiously, and for the most part without incident. The eccentrics in those films are bent to the norm, mainstreamers just waiting for an excuse to come out. The truth of southern Indiana is in a lack of norm, a place full of idiots and savants alike, sometimes collapsed into the same people, wonderful whacko fruitcakes and nut cases that the terrain tolerates, sustains, even endures, almost in sanctuary terms. There are real-life equivalents for all the Compsons and other families created by Faulkner. They don't live in notoriety. Often, you miss them if you blink.

My Bloomington experience was full of getting out of the city and getting lost in the many kinds of countryside. A log cabin, an entire log cabin in the woods between Bloomington and Nashville in Brown County, could be had in the early 1970s for the rental of fifty dollars a month. Lake Lemon was out there in the same direction, always a safe and staid place full of sailboats and patchwork volleyball games. Lake Monroe was out there in the same direction, more of an adventure than Lake Lemon, with nature paths, camping, faster boating, and people who had picnics out of the trunks of their cars, the way poorer tourists do on Maui or Muscle Beach. But the more adventuresome found Lost Lake or went to Crooked Creek.

The exotic became the commonplace in this landscape. You could go up in air balloons or go spelunking, you could go on turkey shoots with bows and arrows, take the tours of several local wineries that have since branched out and made their fortunes in Napa Valley. You could stop in at any of several closet-sized dives and diners that advertised "home cooking," you could be dressed in tie-dye T-shirt and wet swimming trunks, and the special might be Lebanese kibbee or Japanese sushi. Dating didn't have to mean a movie and beer in a bar in town. Often, I took women I barely knew for drives in the country, only to stop where we found bonfires or heard guitars playing, throw a blanket in a cornfield, or sneak up a ladder to the hayloft of some farmer's barn.

I never got my fill of Indiana. Graduate school went by too quickly, and I was forced to spend a lot of my student time there in the library, in classes, in my room writing my dissertation. But when I packed my car to move to Philadelphia and take my first teaching job, I didn't have to turn around or look back, because I knew I would be coming back, more a spiritual need than a self-fulfilling prophecy.

I had met my wife in graduate school in Bloomington. She remembered Indiana bleakly: the lack of light during winter months, the depressing sameness of fried foods and heavy starches in dorm cafeterias, the stiff pedantry of some of her teachers, the painful process of her dissertation. She remembered southern Indiana as the birthplace of the KKK, the Vietnam War as a thorny reminder of the outside world, and she spoke of Hoosiers disdainfully. She felt in some way "delivered" by having met me, glad that our marriage was taking us away, and she was in no hurry to go back.

Our marriage lasted ten years, and during that time Indiana was not our getaway place. But when the marriage collapsed and I found myself the single parent of three small boys, all under the age of five, I resolved never to spend a full summer in Philadelphia but instead to take the boys on trips back to Michigan to spend time around my father, my brothers and sisters, other people who looked like me and claimed me, so they could have some sense of extended family and I could have some mental relief from the *single* part of single-parenting.

There's a more direct route from Philadelphia to Michigan than going through southern Indiana, but our yearly swings have always included stay-overs in Bloomington, both on the way there and on the way back. I have often wondered why. Maybe it was a place I felt good in and safe enough to take chances, and I wanted to pass that on to my boys. Maybe, on the other hand, I needed to go back there to "exorcise" that part of southern Indiana I had shared with my wife as a way to get over my divorce and move on with my emotional life. More likely, it was a kind of halfway house, a place to slough off Pennsylvania and get ready emotionally for Michigan or a place, having left the lake in Michigan, to stall returning to the dog days of Philadelphia in August.

Whatever the psychic reasons, I went back, not as a would-be graduate student again (I avoided going to the university buildings) or as a tour guide for my kids to do nostalgia, and definitely not as someone just passing through, but rather as a bona fide Hoosier, even though I couldn't speak that twang and had no real estate to make my claim. The landscape was still mine for the taking, the memories I once had gave way to gradually accumulating memories of things done in previous summers with my boys, *our* memories. There were certain stops I would always want to make, Rorschach stops by anyone's rational calculations: eating a Hinkleburger, looking into the old Salvation Army surplus store, checking out what films were playing at the Von Lee, stopping at Bryan Park for a game of baseball. But these stops took less and less time each summer until finally I forgot to make most of them. They were like the tonsils or appendix of an earlier time, a former body, someone else than the father I now was to these boys.

The boys have their own memories, their own highlights film in their minds. One summer their favorite thing to do was to go up and down Browncliff Road at my friend Nancy's and sometimes all the way down to Griffey Lake and back, catching fireflies (or lightning bugs) and putting them in a jar, watching their lights go on and off for hours, then setting them free again when it was bedtime. Another summer's major theme was the setting off of all the elaborate fireworks we had bought in Ohio. Another summer meant searching out all the waterslides and flumes. Other summers came to be known for skateboarding, baseball card shows, horses, hitting golf balls at the IU practice range.

During all of these visits, it seemed to me that my sons began to look like boys of summer, Hoosier boys of summer, with flattop or pixie haircuts, cherub cheeks, good smiles well met, and farmer's tans on arms and legs. They softened up from their big-city vigilance, stopped rolling up the windows and locking the car doors when we parked somewhere, stopped looking suspiciously at strangers. They stayed up later and got up earlier, both more refreshed and more in a daze, both at once, if that's possible. They swore boredom, but they didn't act bored. I could leave them or they could leave me for long stretches of time, without any wondering where the other was. I overheard them telling friends back East that their vast wealth when they grew up would include a summer home in southern Indiana.

I feel healed now. I envy people who live all-year-round in southern Indiana, some of whom probably envy me my lifestyle in the East, grasses always being greener. I went to Indiana the first time a fresh-faced know-it-all boy, someone about on the edge of not being teachable, I thought I knew so much. Twenty years later, I'm still going back. I was the loneliest I've ever been in Indiana. Growing up proved to be much harder than getting a degree. I left Indiana because of the Vietnam War and came back afterward, that war splitting me into two people, the one who left scared and angry, the other who came back grateful and determined. Beyond all the classes in foreign languages, the film courses and photography courses, beyond all the academic work

I did there, what I learned in Indiana was that I had a body, a man's body I had to come to terms with, ways of holding my body, expressing my body, nurturing the body. I've long ago forgotten much of my course work but not the lessons of the body. Wherever we do that body work is "home" to us, whether we live there or not. These places may seem magical in the mind, the memories that only seem to reside in the mind, but in fact whatever magic they hold has to do with the power they give to the body: a shift in posture, a deep breath, a learned way of looking long and soft at something. Here and only here do we allow ourselves to feel melancholy as a good thing, to feel God as something more than faith, to grow old gracefully. Indiana is more than the place where I got my doctorate and met my future wife. It's the place where boyhood pain and confusion got sorted out, where who I have become first started happening, where all the contradictions got energized and, while remaining contradictions, got elevated to a place beyond polarities of multiple truths and inner peace. I can't imagine a tour book whose descriptions of southern Indiana would ever dissuade people from going to Fisherman's Wharf or the Grand Canyon or even Disney World. Words won't do it. And I still smile when people preach the "horrors" of the Heartland, the flatness as a disease, the farms as a mind-blindness, the sturdy people as some kind of disaster of stunted personality types. I don't even try to convince them. My heartland and theirs are as different as, say, being *on* the Golden Gate Bridge and looking down versus having a postcard. Apples and oranges. It's like some best-kept secret, one that's right out there in the open, plain as day, the hidden Troy underneath Turkey. The body knows what it knows and it ain't talking.